CHRIST
and his
PEOPLE
in the book of Isaiah

DAVID PETERSON

Inter-Varsity Press

INTER-VARSITY PRESS
38 De Montfort Street, Leicester LE1 7GP, England
Email: ivp@uccf.org.uk
Website: www.ivpbooks.com

First published 2003

British Library Cataloguing in Publication Data
A catalogue record for this book is available from the British Library.

ISBN 0–85111–689–2

Set in 10.5 / 14 Dante
Typeset in Great Britain by Saffron Page Ltd, Norwich
Printed in Great Britain by Creative Print & Design Group, Ebbw Vale

Inter-Varsity Press is the publishing division of the Universities and Colleges Christian Fellowship (formerly the Inter-Varsity Fellowship), a student movement linking Christian Unions in universities and colleges throughout Great Britain, and a member movement of the International Fellowship of Evangelical Students. For more information about local and national activities write to UCCF, 38 De Montfort Street, Leicester LE1 7GP, email us at email@uccf.org.uk, or visit the UCCF website at www.uccf.org.uk.

Contents

To Lesley, my wife,
in gratitude for our marriage
and partnership in the gospel

Introduction

The genesis of this book was a series of sermons preached in the chapel of Oak Hill Theological College, London. Staff and students had been engaged in ongoing discussion about a Christ-centred approach to the interpretation of the Old Testament. Questions were being asked about whether passages could have a different meaning for Old Testament believers and for Christians today, about appropriate ways of making a Christian application, and about the degree to which Old Testament believers could have had a trust in Christ and his work.

It seemed important to offer a model of how I would approach a critical part of Isaiah's prophecy, preaching it as the living word of God to a Christian congregation, while taking proper account of the original context in which the material was first delivered. Some of the material has subsequently been preached in ordinary church situations.

What follows is not a detailed commentary on these chapters. I list below the commentaries that I found most helpful in my preparation. I have also not simply given a written version of my sermons. My views about preaching are briefly outlined in chapter 1. Even the best of commentaries give only hints about how to expound and apply Old Testament passages to Christians. They concentrate on textual and historical matters, and give broad indications of the theological issues involved in various contexts. When they offer guidance for Christian application of the material, it is often related to specific verses or themes, rather than to whole passages.

There are also books that explore the issue of preaching the Old Testament more theoretically. I have found the works of Sidney Greidanus and Graeme Goldsworthy particularly helpful and explain in my first chapter how I am indebted to their insights. These writers discuss particular problems related to different literary genres and offer brief examples of how to expound various passages from the Old Testament. However, they do not show how to deal with passages in detail or demonstrate how to unfold the message of a succession of chapters in a biblical book.

So this examination of key chapters in Isaiah's prophecy seeks to bridge the gap between commentaries, books about preaching and sermons. I have not always taken the application as far as I might in addressing a congregation, but have indicated directions I might take. Sometimes the application sections are longer because I challenge popular ways of approaching the text or because the unfolding of its message in the New Testament is complex and needs to be understood at different levels.

My hope is that this little book will be helpful to preachers and others who lead Bible studies or teach Scripture in other contexts. Some may find it helpful for devotional reading. My goal is to bring these passages to life as a model, hoping that some of the principles and conclusions might help with the interpretation of other Old Testament prophecies. Some may feel it impossible to preach large segments of Isaiah but may feel encouraged to take smaller bites than I have chosen. I am grateful for comments on various sections of my work received from Barry Webb, James Robson and Joel Edwards.

The new English Standard Version of the Bible (ESV) has been quoted from throughout and is the basis of the exposition. This is because of its normally more literal approach to the translation of the Hebrew. Where relevant, I have compared other translations such as the New International Version (NIV), and tried to explain significant differences.

Recommended commentaries

In the following chapters, these works will be referred to simply by the author's surname.

E. J. Young, *The Book of Isaiah*, Vol. 1 (Grand Rapids, MI: Eerdmans, 1965), chs. 1 – 18

J. N. Oswalt, *The Book of Isaiah Chapters 1 – 39*, The New International Commentary on the Old Testament (Grand Rapids, MI: Eerdmans, 1986)

J. A. Motyer, *The Prophecy of Isaiah* (Leicester: Inter-Varsity Press, 1993)

B. Webb, *The Message of Isaiah*, The Bible Speaks Today (Leicester: Inter-Varsity Press, 1996)

J. Goldingay, *Isaiah, New International Biblical Commentary* (Peabody, MA: Hendrickson; Carlisle: Paternoster, 2001)

David Peterson

1 Preaching Christ from the Old Testament

Many Christians find it difficult to discern the relevance of the Old Testament to their own life-situation. Even those who have been theologically trained may avoid the Old Testament in their teaching or give poor models of interpretation in the way they handle the text. Some hurry on from the literal, historical meaning to a spiritual sense, giving little indication of what the passage might have meant to those who first received it. The relevance of the text to contemporary life becomes the controlling agenda. A direct and personal application is what they are seeking.

Some use the Old Testament merely as a launching pad for expounding biblical themes. Doctrinal application becomes of paramount importance and the Bible's story-line is ignored. Some allegorize incidental features of the text in their desire to be relevant, but miss the central implications of the passage for an understanding of Christ and his work.

At the other extreme, there are those who have been influenced by certain traditions of Old Testament scholarship, who doubt that there is any unity in the Bible or any progressive revelation culminating in the Lord Jesus Christ. They consider that a Christocentric interpretation of Old Testament texts is illegitimate or dangerous, imposing a grid over the text that distorts its meaning.

We know that Jesus spent much time explaining to his disciples 'what was said in all the Scriptures concerning himself' (Luke 24:27). Particularly in the period after his resurrection, he opened their minds so they could understand the Scriptures and proclaimed: 'Everything must be fulfilled that is written about me in the Law of Moses, the Prophets and the Psalms' (Luke 24:44). To his opponents he said: 'You diligently search the Scripture because you think that by them you possess eternal life. These are the Scriptures that testify about me, yet you refuse to come to me to have life' (John 5:39–40).

As disciples of Christ, following his lead, we should be constantly looking for ways in which the Old Testament testifies to him. The New Testament shows how the earliest Christians explored the Christological significance of a great range of Old Testament texts.[1] We are encouraged by their example to interpret the Old Testament in the light of its fulfilment, in a way that leads people to Jesus as Saviour and Lord. Putting it another way, the Old Testament cannot simply be considered in isolation, in a purely historical sense, but we are challenged by Jesus and his apostles to discover its Christian significance.

This raises some big questions, however. How much did people in Old Testament times know about the Christ? How much were they expected to know at different stages in the unfolding of God's plan of redemption? How should we interpret a passage with relevance to its original context, while putting Christ and his work in centre place? Should every biblical study or sermon on the Old Testament have a specifically Christological focus or outcome? Isn't there a danger of reading things into the text that were never intended by the human authors? Isn't there a danger that all Christocentric expositions of the Old Testament will sound more or less the same?

---

1. R. N. Longenecker, *Biblical Exegesis in the Apostolic Period* (Grand Rapids, MI: Eerdmans, 1975), is a good introduction to this topic.

Establishing some ground rules

Ever since New Testament times, there have been different ways in which Christians have interpreted and applied the Old Testament. Some methods have been carefully considered and argued, but others have been arbitrary or individual, and not well defended. Some have been driven by distinctive theological or philosophical agendas, rather than by the character and shape of Scripture itself. Is there any way to establish some ground rules for Christian preachers and teachers to follow?

Greidanus's approach

Sidney Greidanus has helpfully surveyed the work of key figures in church history, to assess the strengths and weaknesses of their solutions to this problem.[2] He then establishes some New Testament principles for preaching Christ from the Old Testament, keeping in mind the results of his historical survey. The method he finally proposes 'falls somewhere between Calvin's theocentric method and Luther's christological method' and is called 'the christocentric method, or, more precisely, the redemptive-historical christocentric method'.[3]

Greidanus suggests a multiplex, rather than a single method of discerning the Christian significance of Old Testament texts. He actually proposes seven ways in which Christ can be preached from the Old Testament. There is some overlap between these methods and often they can be used in combination. In the chapters that follow, I will draw attention to the relevance of some of these principles for the interpretation of Isaiah 6 – 12. I list them below, with a brief description of what is meant in each case, but would urge those who

---

2. S. Greidanus, *Preaching Christ from the Old Testament: A Contemporary Hermeneutical Method* (Grand Rapids, MI, and Cambridge, UK: Eerdmans, 1999), pp. 69–176.

3. Ibid., p. 227.

want to think this issue through to read Greidanus for themselves.

1. *The way of redemptive-historical progression.* This is 'the bedrock for preaching Christ from the Old Testament'. It means placing every passage in the broad context of redemptive history, which culminates in Christ and the ultimate rule of God over a restored and transformed creation. This involves understanding the point in redemptive history when the revelation is given and considering how the passage relates to what has gone before, as well as to what will follow in the unfolding plan of God.

2. *The way of promise-fulfilment.* Biblical prophecy is fulfilled progressively – in instalments, as it were. In interpreting the text, it is important to move from the promise of the Old Testament to the fulfilment in Christ and back again to the Old Testament text, to determine more clearly how the word was fulfilled, is being fulfilled and will be fulfilled.

3. *The way of typology.* Typology functions within Scripture because God is sovereign over redemptive history and acts in regular patterns. So New Testament writers discern analogies between God's acts in Christ and his redemptive acts in the Old Testament. But typology involves more than analogy or drawing parallels. It implies development, escalation and consummation, sometimes also contrast (as with Adam and Christ in Romans 5). People and events in the Old Testament are regarded as shadows or prefigurations of what has now been realized in Christ.[4]

4. *The way of analogy.* Old Testament narrators frequently highlight the continuities in biblical history by 'casting later events and persons more or less in the image of earlier events and persons'. New Testament writers also use analogy to establish 'the continuity and progression in God's dealings with Israel and through Christ with the Church'. They apply to Jesus and the church passages that speak about God acting in relation to his people Israel. Such passages

---

4. The Greek word *typos*, from which we get 'typology', can mean 'pattern', 'model' (cf. Acts 7:44; Rom. 5:14; Heb. 8:5) or 'example' (cf. 1 Cor. 10:6, 11).

are not specifically 'messianic' in their original context.

5. *The way of longitudinal themes.* Various themes that are traced through the Old Testament, such as covenant, redemption, sacrifice and holiness, are picked up in the New Testament and reinterpreted in the light of Christ.

6. *The way of New Testament references.* Many New Testament references to Old Testament passages evidence the ways of promise-fulfilment, typology or longitudinal themes. Sometimes they suggest unexpected and productive links with Old Testament figures and events. Sometimes they use methods of interpretation that may not be normative for today, and Greidanus offers various cautions in this regard.[5] This is a controversial issue, which necessitates a careful consideration of the way in which certain Old Testament texts are used in the New Testament.

7. *The way of contrast.* Preceding methods focus on the continuity between the Old and New Testaments, even though they recognize development and fulfilment in Christ. Sometimes, however, the New Testament notes major differences in the way God achieves his kingdom purposes or relates to his people in Christ. We need to understand the discontinuity that Christ brings.

Goldsworthy's approach

A different examination of this issue is offered by Graeme Goldsworthy. He takes a redemptive-historical approach to Scripture like Greidanus, but argues more emphatically that 'all texts in the whole Bible bear a discernible relationship to Christ and are primarily intended as testimony to Christ'.[6] Old Testament passages should not be applied simply and directly to New

---

5. Greidanus, *Preaching Christ*, pp. 185–191.

6. G. Goldsworthy, *Preaching the Whole Bible as Christian Scripture: The Application of Biblical Theology to Expository Preaching* (Grand Rapids, MI: Eerdmans; Leicester: Inter-Varsity Press, 2000), p. 113.

Testament believers. First we must ask how the text applies to the person and work of Christ. Then we can begin to see how it applies to Christians through Christ or because of Christ.

This is such an important point that it needs to be explained more fully. The interpreter must first understand how an Old Testament text functions in its literary and historical context. But it is also important to determine its context within salvation history. In other words, what is going on theologically at this point in the Bible's story? The essential framework for establishing the structure and high points of salvation history is the gospel of Jesus and his apostles.[7] The whole Bible must be understood in the light of God's final Word in Jesus Christ, which explains everything that leads up to it.

Goldsworthy speaks of different 'epochs' in the progress of salvation history. Characters or institutions in the text need to be examined 'for their theological function in the epoch to which they belong',[8] before being related to Christ and his work. Goldsworthy describes those epochs in the following way.

- Genesis 4 – 11 is the prologue to salvation history.
- There is then a progressive revelation of salvation and the kingdom of God in the epoch from Abraham to David.
- In the epoch from Solomon to the end of the Old Testament, there is a progressive decline of the kingdoms of Israel and Judah under judgment. However, during this period the prophets speak of the coming salvation and kingdom of God as a more glorious 'recapitulation of what has happened in the past history of Israel'.[9]

---

7. Cf. ibid., p. 98. The New Testament concentrates on certain parts of the Old Testament, 'but this does not relieve us of the task of seeking to understand the function of the less prominent parts' (p. 102).

8. Ibid., p. 114.

9. Ibid., p. 107.

- In the New Testament epoch, Jesus Christ is declared to be the fulfiller of those expectations. 'He is the solid reality of which the history and prophetic expressions are the foreshadowing.'[10]

Goldsworthy expounds a typology based on the principle that 'people, events and institutions in the Old Testament correspond to, and foreshadow, other people, events or institutions that come later'.[11] The New Testament gives certain examples of such typology, encouraging us to look more widely for typological links when we are reading the Old Testament. However, Goldsworthy also discerns in the Bible what he calls 'a macro-typology that is far-reaching in its application'.[12] There are correspondences between whole epochs of revelation. For example, the idea that God saves his people in order to rule over them and to make them a blessing to others is a common theme in each epoch. This is expressed in various ways in those epochs, culminating in the person and work of Christ.

When we come to the application of an Old Testament text, the point of contact with our contemporary situation is first and foremost the Lord Jesus Christ. So, for example, passages about the role and significance of the tabernacle or temple in the plan of God cannot be applied simply and directly to the church. Christ himself is pre-eminently the 'place' to meet with God and see his glory (cf. John 1:14; 2:19–22). Jesus replaces the temple at Jerusalem as the source of life and renewal for the world and he himself is the promised centre for the ingathering of the nations (cf. John 12:32). Temple imagery can be applied to Christians only because they are joined to Christ by faith. We have been 'built together into a dwelling place for God' by the Spirit poured out by Christ (cf. Eph.

---

10. Ibid., p. 109.
11. Ibid., p. 109.
12. Ibid., p. 111.

2:19–22; I Cor. 3:16–17; 2 Cor. 6:6–18).[13]

Greidanus and Goldsworthy compared

Once again, I would urge those who want to think this issue through to read Goldsworthy for themselves and compare his approach with that of Greidanus. I find myself very much influenced by the gospel-driven approach of Goldsworthy. This mirrors the apostolic preaching in Acts, which I briefly discuss at the end of this chapter, and the Christocentric use of the Old Testament elsewhere in the New Testament. I particularly appreciate his insistence that the interpretation of an Old Testament text must proceed theologically, via the application it has to Christ.

Goldsworthy's insistence that the theme of the Bible as a whole is the kingdom of God assures me that, when I am reading about God fulfilling his purpose for Israel, or Israelites being challenged to respond to such initiatives, or judged for not responding, I am in touch with kingdom structures of thought. There is ultimately an application to Christ and his people from all such passages. The gospel is the hermeneutical key to unlock the meaning of Scripture as a whole.

However, we must avoid the kind of reductionism or over-simplification that makes a limited range of applications from Old Testament texts. The aim is not just to preach the gospel from every passage. We have much to learn about the character and purpose of God as a foundation for understanding the gospel and its application to our lives. 'The biblical prophetic books contain more than eschatology, and preaching from the prophets can involve us in a wide range of perspectives and topics.'[14] Furthermore, the theology of the kingdom of God allows me to have a theocentric approach to the Old Testament that does not

---

13. Cf. D. G. Peterson, *Engaging with God: A Biblical Theology of Worship* (Leicester: Apollos; Downers Grove: IVP, 1992), pp. 93–102, 200–205.

14. Goldsworthy, *Preaching the Whole Bible*, p. 167.

always move immediately to a Christological resolution. The challenge is not to read Christ into the Old Testament but to show how characters, institutions and events prepare for, anticipate and illuminate the significance of Christ and his work.

Greidanus offers several routes to New Testament application, though the way of redemptive-historical progression is clearly foundational for him. He offers a more complex and eclectic approach than Goldsworthy, opening up some exciting and varied lines of interpretation. In the expositions that follow, I explore some of the pathways to application he suggests. The problem with Greidanus's approach is determining which 'way' to follow and deciding which line of interpretation should take priority. He does not show us the link between these perspectives, other than to say that they centre on Christ. I also think he is over-cautious in the matter of typology, ruling out the typological application of persons, institutions or events in the Old Testament that are not symbolic in the narrative in which they are found.[15]

Here I believe the macro-typology propounded by Goldsworthy is particularly helpful. This reveals more clearly the underlying unity of Scripture, the structure of redemptive history and the way all things are summed up in Christ. As I have tested various options suggested by Greidanus, I have found myself finally guided by the gospel-driven approach of Goldsworthy.

Isaiah 6 – 12

Isaiah 6 – 12 is critical for understanding the book of Isaiah and the prophetic epoch which prepares for the coming of the messianic

---

15. E.g. Greidanus, *Preaching Christ*, p. 258. He is right to say that the link of redness between Rahab's cord and Christ's blood is spurious. But the cord symbolized something, for by its display Rahab and her family were saved. We are justified in asking, from a Christological or gospel perspective, what this might represent for us.

salvation. Certain passages, such as Isaiah 9:6–7, speak so obviously about the Lord Jesus Christ. But what do we do with the earlier verses in this chapter and their unusual claims? What do we make of the surrounding chapters and how do we fit that particular prophecy into the wider context of Isaiah's predictions? How do we proceed from the prophet's call in Isaiah 6 to Christ? How do we relate the warnings of judgment in Isaiah 9:8 – 10:34 to Christ?

An important 'text plot'

New Testament writers appear to have been particularly influenced by certain blocks of Old Testament material in explaining the person and work of Christ. There is reason to believe that Jesus himself directed the minds of his first followers to such contexts or 'text plots', so that they might 'find illumination upon the meaning of his mission and destiny'.[16]

Isaiah 6 – 12 is one of those text plots, because quotations from these chapters are found in many New Testament books. The following chart lists direct citations, but does not take into account allusions such as 'the root of David' (Rev. 5:5; 22:16; cf. Is. 11:1, 10) or

---

Direct quotations from Isaiah 6 – 12

Isaiah 6:9–10 in Matthew 13:14–15 (cf. Mark 4:12; Luke 8:10); John 12:40; Acts 28:26–27

Isaiah 7:14 in Matthew 1:23

Isaiah 8:14 in 1 Peter 2:8 (cf. Romans 9:32–33)

Isaiah 8:17–18 in Hebrews 2:13

Isaiah 9:1–2 in Matthew 4:15–16

Isaiah 10:22–23 in Romans 9:27–28

Isaiah 11:10 in Romans 15:12

---

16. C. H. Dodd, *According to the Scriptures: The Sub-Structure of New Testament Theology* (London: Nisbet, 1952), p. 110. Dodd included Isaiah 6:1 – 9:7; 11:1–10 amongst what he called 'Scriptures of the New Israel'.

verbal links between the visions in Isaiah 6 and the Revelation to John.

Tracing the way those quotations are used by New Testament writers will be a particularly fruitful way of understanding how to apply Isaiah's prophecies today. But a proper understanding of the context from which they come will enable us to make further connections. Indeed, Isaiah 6 – 12 gives us a framework for understanding God's purposes for the world, as the prophet views the present and the future in the light of God's dealings with Israel in the past.

The perspective of these chapters

Isaiah 6 – 12 belongs to the epoch from Solomon to the end of the Old Testament, when there is a progressive decline of the kingdoms of Israel and Judah under judgment. However, during this period the prophets speak of the coming salvation and kingdom of God as a more glorious recapitulation of what has happened in the past.

Isaiah proclaims a terrible divine judgment on the divided kingdom of Israel at the hands of the Assyrians. His immediate concern is with events in the eighth century BC. There is a particular focus on the failure of the kings in Jerusalem descended from David. Their commission was to rule in a way that enabled Israel to fulfil its destiny as the covenant people of God. Into this gloomy picture Isaiah shines a ray of hope. This hope is related to the Assyrian crisis but, from a New Testament perspective, incorporates events associated with the first and second comings of Christ. This is so because of the central importance of the Messiah to these chapters.

Isaiah promises that God will enable a remnant of Israel to survive, to be the nucleus of his renewed people. The re-establishment of God's purposes for Israel and the nations will be linked to the arrival of the new king from David's line. His rule will be different from any before: it will be eternal and will be characterized by wisdom, righteousness, justice and peace. Indeed, his rule will bring about the reversal of all the evil consequences of humanity's rebellion against God, establishing a new creation.

At one level, these chapters echo some of the messages emerging from other prophetic ministries in ancient Israel.[17] Amos 9:11–15, for example, contains some of the same ideas in a more embryonic form:

> 'In that day I will raise up
>> the booth of David that is fallen,
> and repair its breaches,
>> and raise up its ruins,
>> and rebuild it as in the days of old,
> that they may possess the remnant of Edom
>> and all the nations who are called by my name,'
>> declares the LORD who does this.
>
> 'Behold the days are coming,' declares the LORD,
> 'when the ploughman shall overtake the reaper,
>> and the treader of grapes him who sows the seed;
> the mountains shall drip sweet wine,
>> and all the hills shall flow with it.
> I will restore the fortunes of my people Israel,
>> and they shall rebuild the ruined cities and inhabit them;
> they shall plant vineyards and drink their wine,
>> and they shall make gardens and eat their fruit.
> I will plant them on their land,
>> and they shall never again be uprooted
>> out of the land that I have given them,'
>>> says the LORD your God.

At another level, Isaiah provides much more detail and exposes the

---

17. Cf. P. E. Satterthwaite, R. S. Hess, G. J. Wenham (eds.), *The Lord's Anointed: Interpretation of Old Testament Messianic Texts* (Carlisle: Paternoster; Grand Rapids, MI: Baker, 1995).

plan of God more extensively. These chapters mark an important new stage in the revelation of God's redemptive purpose and demonstrate the centrality of the Messiah to its accomplishment. Christians who want to understand how the Bible fits together need to have a good understanding of these critical prophecies.

Preaching 'the whole counsel of God'

The following chapters assume that systematic exposition of biblical passages is the best way to preach Scripture in the church today. There is less chance of verses being taken out of context or of doctrinal agendas controlling the interpretation of the text. Each week in a series brings a clearer understanding of the message of the book being studied. Congregations are taught how to handle the Bible for themselves and their general knowledge of Scripture and its themes is gradually built up. Systematic exposition of Scripture still allows for thematic preaching, with a doctrinal, evangelistic or ethical focus determined by the content of the passage in question.

My own approach to teaching the Bible in this way is first to discover the structure, flow and intention of a given passage within its immediate literary and historical context. In so doing, I try to put myself in the position of the people originally addressed and seek to understand what God was saying to them. However, it is also important to understand the significance of characters, institutions and events within the structure of the biblical revelation as a whole. My concern is always to understand the theological context and significance of a passage.

Guidelines from Acts

In this connection, it is interesting to reflect on the early Christian preaching recorded in the Acts of the Apostles. Teaching about the way Scripture has been fulfilled in Christ was an important part of the apostolic proclamation of the gospel (e.g. 2:16–39; 8:30–35; 13:16–41; 17:2–3). But it was also essential for the nurturing and maturing of the church. Reflecting on his unusually lengthy period of ministry in Ephesus, the apostle Paul uses various terms to describe what he did (20:18–32).

He firstly speaks about teaching 'in public and from house to house, testifying both to Jews and to Greeks of repentance towards God and of faith in our Lord Jesus Christ' (vv. 20–21). In other words, there was a clear proclamation of Jesus as Lord and Messiah, with an urgent appeal to turn to God and to trust in Jesus as the one sent to fulfil his plan for Israel and the nations. Another way of describing this is 'to testify to the gospel of the grace of God' (v. 24). However, the wider biblical framework of his teaching is more clearly revealed when he speaks of 'proclaiming the kingdom' (v. 25).

This was Jesus' preferred way of speaking about the gospel and its implications (e.g. Mark 1:14–15; 4:11; 9:1; 10:14–15, 23, 25). In the early church, the kingdom of God continued to be a convenient short-hand way of summarizing the message proclaimed by his disciples (Acts 8:12; 19:8; 20:25; 28:23, 31). Although the term 'kingdom of God' does not appear as such in the Old Testament, the concept of God's rule or sovereignty over creation and human history is absolutely foundational.

- The rejection of God's rule by the human race brought disastrous consequences (Gen. 3 – 11), but the rest of the Old Testament is about the way God acts to reverse that situation.
- God's covenant initiative with Abraham holds the promise of salvation under the rule of God for Israel and the nations (Gen. 12:1–3).
- The outworking of God's covenant promises in Israel's history is the background for Isaiah's words of judgment and his predictions about the future.
- The coming of the Messiah is decisive for the establishment of God's rule over Israel and the nations in a renewed creation.

So Paul's preaching of Christ and the facts of the gospel was set within the wider theological framework of 'proclaiming the kingdom'. Another term, which probably describes this same approach, is 'declaring to you the whole counsel of God' (Acts 20:27). The Greek word translated 'counsel' (*boulē*) suggests that he gave them an understanding of the plan or purpose of God as revealed in Scripture. This doubtless included an explanation of the big picture from particular texts, such as we see in Romans 9 – 11.

Proclaiming the kingdom from Isaiah 6 – 12

Preaching from a section of a prophetic book such as Isaiah 6 – 12 is a way of proclaiming the kingdom of God or teaching 'the whole counsel of God'. Christians are introduced to a major biblical prophet and shown how God addressed his people at a particular point of crisis in their history. At the same time, it is possible to see from these chapters how God was preparing his people for the fulfilment of his plan for Israel and the whole world in the sending of the Messiah and the establishment of his kingdom. Here is a way of looking backwards and forwards, to see the outworking of God's plan from beginning to end.

Application of such passages to Christ and his people enables us to hear the gospel being proclaimed and to receive the exhortation or appeal of God to respond in a variety of situations. There is a breadth of material in the prophetic literature that makes it possible to relate the gospel to a range of personal, social and political contexts in our own time. The inspiration, unity and authority of Scripture are practically demonstrated and pastorally experienced as these ancient texts are expounded in the light of God's ultimate purpose for us in Christ.

2   Who is the True King?
(Isaiah 6)

'The king is dead, long live the king!' This famous expression indicates the end of one era and the beginning of another, the death of one ruler and the inauguration of his successor. Perhaps similar words were uttered in the year that Uzziah, king of Jerusalem, died. A prosperous fifty-two-year reign and a period of co-regency with his son Jotham (2 Kgs. 15:5) gave stability, peace and a sense of confidence to the people of Judah. Jotham would continue for only a short while (740/39–732/31), but would be followed by his son Ahaz (732/31–716/15). There were threatening developments on the international scene, but the continuation of Uzziah's dynasty seemed to provide assurance that all would be well.

So it is for nations today, whose welfare is dependent on the continuation of a particular system of leadership, whether constitutional monarchy or elected presidency. Politics looms large in our thinking because it offers the possibility of wealth, security, good health and long life. Human leaders assume great significance for us, because we recognize that so much depends on them. But where does God fit into the picture? How much does our reliance on stable government and strong direction from relevant authorities obscure the kingship of God and our dependence on him? Dependence on human wisdom and ingenuity is the only alternative for those who do not know the power and purpose of God.

Into the relative calm and stability of Jotham's reign, God sent the prophet Isaiah with words of challenge and judgment (Is. 1 – 5). His call and commission, which surprisingly come in Isaiah 6 rather than at the beginning of the book, show how God was confronting both prophet and people with the reality of divine kingship.[1] The chapter forms a hinge between the opening oracles and what is to follow in Isaiah 7 – 12. What we are to explore in those chapters is 'a fulfillment and an explication of the word given to Isaiah in his call' (Oswalt).

While Isaiah 6 has important things to say about the nature of Isaiah's ministry and about the way God would use him to establish his kingly purpose, the focus is on the character of God and what it means to know him as the Holy One. More specifically, from a Christian point of view, this chapter raises questions about the way God's glory is revealed and his rule is established through the person and work of the Lord Jesus Christ.

1. The holiness of the true king (Is. 6:1–7)

[1]In the year that King Uzziah died I saw the Lord sitting upon a throne, high and lifted up; and the train of his robe filled the temple. [2]Above him stood the seraphim. Each had six wings: with two he covered his face, and with two he covered his feet, and with two he flew. [3]And one called to another and said:

---

1. Isaiah 1 – 5 introduces the prophet's general message, before Isaiah 6 introduces the prophet himself. This delayed account of the call to prophetic office highlights Isaiah's authority to speak as he does and reinforces what has already been proclaimed. It shows that the prophet was essentially driven by a conviction of God's sovereignty and holiness,

'Holy, holy, holy is the Lord of hosts;
the whole earth is full of his glory!'

[4]And the foundations of the thresholds shook at the voice of him who called, and the house was filled with smoke. [5]And I said: 'Woe is me! For I am lost; for I am a man of unclean lips, and I dwell in the midst of a people of unclean lips; for my eyes have seen the King, the LORD of hosts!'

[6]Then one of the seraphim flew to me, having in his hand a burning coal that he had taken with tongs from the altar. [7]And he touched my mouth and said: 'Behold, this has touched your lips; your guilt is taken away, and your sin atoned for.'

The date of Uzziah's death is uncertain. Estimates vary from 742 to 735 BC, though 740/39 is favoured by many scholars. A glowing account of his reign is given in 2 Chronicles 26:1–15.[2] His military achievements, his building projects and his programme of agricultural development signified great power and success. In fact, there had been no king like him since the days of Solomon. Like Solomon, he too became proud and unfaithful and experienced the judgment of God in his own personal life (2 Chr. 26:16–23). But the people of Judah as a whole were complacent in their prosperity and rebellion against God, as Isaiah 1 – 5 reveals. Little did they know that 'the great glory and national pride of Judah were now facing an end, never to rise again' (Young).

It was in the critical year of Uzziah's death, then, that Isaiah 'saw the Lord sitting upon a throne, high and lifted up'. What he 'saw' was not with the bodily eye, for God is invisible and cannot be seen by mortals directly (cf. Exod. 33:18–23; John 1:18; 1 Tim. 6:16). The

which was given to him at the time of this unique vision.

2. The briefer account in 2 Kgs. 15:1–7 calls him Azariah, though the name Uzziah is also used in 2 Kgs. 15:13, 30, 32, 34. Perhaps one was a birth name and one was a throne name.

vision that was given to him was adapted to his capabilities as a finite creature. What he 'saw' was 'the Lord' (literally 'the Sovereign'),[3] 'the absolute overlord of the earth with whom all people have to do' (Oswalt). And he saw him 'high and lifted up', meaning that the Lord is '*high* in his own nature, *exalted*/ "lifted up" by the acknowledgment of his sovereignty' (Motyer).[4]

Isaiah saw the Lord in human form, 'sitting upon a throne, high and lifted up; and the train of his robe filled the temple'. In other words, he saw God as the true king upon his 'throne', with a 'robe' of office and various attendants in his throne room. The glory and majesty of the Lord were portrayed in terms that were recognizable from earthly monarchy, but which clearly indicated his surpassing greatness and power as the transcendent Lord of all. To some extent, the vision reflects details of the temple in Jerusalem, but it cannot be confined to that context. Isaiah is shown the heavenly throne room, to which the earthly temple pointed (cf. 1 Kgs. 8:27–30; Heb. 8:4–6; Rev. 4). 'The Jerusalem temple expands into its heavenly counterpart' (Webb).

'Sitting upon a throne, high and lifted up', the Lord is revealed as exalted king and judge. The fact that 'the train of his robe filled the temple' suggests that his own glory fills the entire space, with no room for anyone to stand in his presence. In preparation for a

---

3. The common Hebrew word for 'Lord' here (*'ăḏōnāy*) is not the personal, covenant name explained to Moses in Exod. 3:13–15 and used in the expression 'the Lord of hosts' in Is. 6:3. That personal name is sometimes represented in English as 'Yahweh', though the Hebrew text indicates that it was never to be pronounced as such but always replaced with the more general word 'Lord'. The difference in Is. 6:1, 8, 11 is that the word *'ăḏōnāy* appears in its own right, not as a substitute for the more personal name.

4. Cf. 52:13; 57:15, where the same paired words refer first to the Servant of the Lord and then again to the Lord himself. The word translated 'lifted up' could mean exalted in the sense of honoured or praised.

ministry in which the sovereign power of God would be displayed and in which his judgment would be proclaimed, Isaiah needed such a revelation of God's majesty.

As in an earthly court, where monarchs have their retinue, the Lord is served by 'the seraphim' (Is. 6:2, lit. 'burning ones'). These are 'personal, spiritual beings, for they have faces, feet and hands, they employ human speech and understand moral concepts' (Young).[5] They stand 'above him', not in any superior way, but apparently waiting to do his will (cf. 1 Kgs. 22:19; Dan. 7:10). Their 'six wings' seem to be important for carrying out their role as God's attendants. Covering 'his face' and 'his feet' suggests humility and reverence before the Lord. 'With two he flew' suggests the function of divine messenger.

a. Holiness and transcendence

The continuous occupation of the seraphim in God's presence is to praise him to one another ('one called to another', Is. 6:3). It is clear that God is as much honoured by such declarations about him as by praise specifically addressed to him (cf. Ps. 145:10–12). They firstly acknowledge his absolute holiness: 'Holy, holy, holy is the LORD of hosts'. Threefold repetition of the word holy is a 'super-superlative', used for great emphasis.[6] In modern English we might say that God is utterly and completely holy.

Isaiah has been described as the prophet of holiness, because the terminology is used so extensively throughout the book bearing his name. Most significantly, God is called 'the Holy One of Israel' twenty-six times, compared with six in the rest of the Old Testament. This distinctive way of speaking about the Lord was presumably

---

5. They appear to be different from 'the living creatures' who surround God's throne in Ezek. 1:22–25; Rev. 4:6–8.

6. This is the only place in the Old Testament where such a threefold repetition is so used. Motyer comments that God's holiness is 'in itself so far beyond human thought that a "super-superlative" has to be invented to express it'. It is possible, though less likely, that this alludes to God as Trinity.

influenced by the extraordinary encounter recorded in Isaiah 6. Motyer suggests that the title is full of majesty and mystery, and yet it is also revealing: 'The God who is transcendent in holiness has brought himself into close relationship with a specified people whereby they may claim that he is theirs and he that they are his.'

The root meaning of holiness is 'separation'.[7] The terminology is used to express the distinctness or otherness of God's character, activities and words. God's holiness is particularly associated with his majesty, sovereignty and awesome power (e.g. Exod. 15:11–12; 19:10–25; Is. 6:1–4). As the one who is supreme over all, he is transcendent, exalted and different from everything he has made. Despite the analogy with human kingship in this vision, God's rule is utterly distinct. Nothing can intervene to hinder his purpose. He is perfectly served by his attendants and does not suffer from corruption and self-interest in his court. He is absolutely sovereign and not even the rebellion of his human subjects can interfere with the fulfilment of his purpose. None of the gods of human imagination can compare with him.

The seraphim also proclaim that 'the whole earth is full of his glory' (Is. 6:3). God's 'glory' in this context is the revelation of his attributes, displayed in the created universe (cf. Rom. 1:19–23). God's holiness cannot be conveyed adequately in vision or word, but it may be encountered in our universe, which is like a vast temple dedicated to his use and the display of his glory. God's glory is his holiness revealed. 'Wherever we turn our eyes, we see the marks of His majesty, and should lift our hearts in praise to Him who is holy' (Young).

b. Holiness and judgment

'And the foundations of the thresholds shook at the voice of him

---

7. The Hebrew root is probably derived from the stem *qd*, 'to cut', rather than from the stems *qd'* or *qdw*, 'to be pure or bright', which are known to us from the Arabic and Ethiopic.

who called, and the house was filled with smoke' (Is. 6:4). Shaking is 'the customary reaction of earth to the divine presence' (Motyer, cf. Exod. 19:18; Hab. 3:3–10). 'Smoke' is also associated with the presence of God in Scripture (Exod. 13:21; 40:34; 1 Kgs. 8:10; Is. 4:5). But what particularly creates the shaking here is 'the voice of him who called' – the call of one seraph to another, as they praised God.

Aware that God's holiness has profound moral implications (Is. 5:16; 35:8; 57:15), the prophet draws back (6:5). What distinguishes the Lord from human beings is not simply his essence but his character. Isaiah knows that God is just and righteous, but he and his people are polluted. God in his holiness must judge all evil and finally remove it from his presence. When the prophet says 'Woe is me!' he means that calamity has fallen or is about to fall on him. When he says 'for I am lost' (lit. 'cut off', 'ruined', 'destroyed'), he means that 'he cannot continue to exist having seen what he has seen' (Oswalt).

The first reason for concluding that he is lost is, 'for I am a man of unclean lips'. The seraphs were praising God with pure lips, but Isaiah knew that he could not join them. Clearly, his 'lips' represent his whole personality, contaminated by sin. Further, he confessed that he dwelt 'in the midst of a people of unclean lips'. He knew himself to be no different from the rest of Israel, who could not worship God acceptably because of their sinfulness (Is. 1:4–15; cf. Ps. 24:3–6).

What made all this so abundantly clear was the fact that, with his own eyes, he had seen the King, the Lord of hosts! This was the second and related reason for concluding that he was 'lost'. He had seen the true sovereign, in his majesty, glory and purity, recognizing him as the covenant Lord of Israel and ruler of everything that exists.

c. Holiness and salvation

How could Isaiah and his people be related to the Holy One and adequately bear witness to his character? The answer comes from

God himself. 'Merciful grace belongs as much to the essence of God's holiness as justice and purity' (Goldingay). Unlike earthly kings, who normally exclude and destroy rebels, the Lord takes the initiative in reconciliation with his enemies. Unlike earthly judges, who can only punish evil, he provides a way of atonement, to restore relationships.

'Then one of the seraphim flew to me, having in his hand a burning coal that he had taken with tongs from the altar' (Is. 6:6). Isaiah is given symbolic assurance that his sins are forgiven. Whether the 'burning coal' was from the altar of sacrifice or the altar of incense is not clear and does not matter. But the true significance of the action is given by the angelic word that follows. 'And he touched my mouth and said: "Behold, this has touched your lips; your guilt is taken away, and your sin atoned for"' (v. 7).

The touching of the 'lips' shows 'how God ministers to the sinner at the point of confessed need' (Motyer). The reality behind this sign is that Isaiah's iniquity or 'guilt' is 'taken away' by God and his 'sin atoned for'. The terminology of the sacrificial system is used to indicate that a comprehensive work of dealing with sin has been effected, though no human act of atonement is implied.[8] Divine forgiveness is based on the removal of sin as an obstacle to fellowship by God himself. In some way, he deals with the problem of sin's penalty. Once we get to Isaiah 53:10–12, it becomes clear that God achieves this through the death of his Servant, whom he makes 'an offering for sin'. The Servant will 'make many to be accounted righteous and he shall bear their iniquities'.

Application
We should be cautious about separating the first part of Isaiah 6 from the second part, because the whole chapter is about the

---

8. Cf. D. Peterson (ed.), *Where Wrath and Mercy Meet: Proclaiming the Atonement Today* (Carlisle: Paternoster, 2001), pp. 1–25, on atonement in the Old Testament.

unique experience of the prophet, as God called and commissioned him. Other biblical figures like Moses and Samuel had received distinctive calls to prophetic ministry before him (cf. Exod. 3; 1 Sam. 3), but such moments in redemptive history were rare. The Lord was preparing Isaiah for his role as authorized messenger in a particular historical situation. 'It was in this encounter with the Lord that Isaiah's understanding of both God and his own mission was crystallized' (Webb).

So the narrative does not challenge us to become prophets or missionaries like Isaiah, but to see him as a unique figure, who was admitted into the divine throne room, to emerge as God's authorized messenger. In relation to Isaiah's message, we must first become 'the audience of prophecy' (Goldingay). We must see God through his eyes and hear God though his ears. The function of the prophets and their writings is to be the means by which God reveals his character and will to his people.

What are we to hear? Isaiah 6 follows the exposure of Israel's sin and the proclamation of divine judgment in the opening chapters. As readers, we are left wondering how Israel can be renewed, to become the centre of blessing for the nations it is destined to be (Is. 2:1–5). How will the Holy One rescue Israel from its pattern of self-destruction and make it the channel of salvation for the rest of the world? Isaiah's experience also challenges us to think about ourselves before God. How can any human being survive in the presence of such a God? Instead of comparing ourselves with others and concluding that we are not too bad after all, we need to see ourselves in the light of God's purity and transcendent majesty.

As New Testament believers, however, we must ask how this revelation relates specifically to God's Son, the Lord Jesus Christ. In this case, we may first be guided by what Greidanus calls 'the way of New Testament references'. John 12:41 tells us that Isaiah saw Christ's glory and spoke about him. In the immediate context, John quotes Isaiah 53:1 ('Lord, who has believed what he heard from us, and to whom has the arm of the Lord been revealed?') and a modified form of Isaiah 6:10 ('He has blinded their eyes and hardened their heart, lest they see with their eyes, and understand with their heart, and turn, and I would heal them').[9]

Both of these texts are chosen because they explain the fundamental problem of Jesus' ministry: 'Though he had done so many signs before them, they still did not believe in him' (John 12:37). John clearly recognizes the element of human sinfulness in this tragedy (e.g. John 1:11; 5:39–47; 8:43–47; 10:31–39). But in John 12:38–41, as elsewhere in this Gospel, he also recognizes God's sovereignty in the process, using the words of Isaiah to make his point.[10]

Such unbelief happened, literally, 'so that the word spoken by the prophet Isaiah might be fulfilled' (John 12:38). John's Greek conveys a strong note of *purpose*. Such unbelief was not only foreseen by Scripture but was also necessitated by it. Isaiah 53:1 refers to the unbelief of the Servant's own people, who despised and rejected him (Is. 53:2–3; cf. Rom. 10:16 in its context). Isaiah's remarkable prediction is that those who 'hear' the good news and 'see' 'the arm of the Lord' revealed in the Servant's life will refuse to believe in him. From John's perspective, 'the arm of the Lord' is particularly revealed in the miraculous signs that Jesus performed, and he views his own generation as the one that fulfils Isaiah's prediction of the

---

9. Most significantly, John 12:40 turns the imperative of Isaiah 6:10 into a statement about what God has done ('He has blinded their eyes and hardened their heart'), to stress God's sovereignty in what happened during the ministry of Jesus. The quotation has also been abbreviated so that Isaiah's reference to 'heart-ears-eyes-eyes-ears-hearts' becomes simply 'eyes-heart-eyes-heart'.

10. Like other biblical writers, when it comes to the question of divine sovereignty and human responsibility, John is philosophically 'a compatibilist', viewing both in operation together. Cf. D. A. Carson, *Divine Sovereignty and Human Responsibility: Biblical Perspectives in Tension* (London: Marshall, Morgan & Scott, 1981).

Servant's rejection and death. Paradoxically, however, it will be the suffering, death and exaltation of the Servant that reveals his true glory and brings salvation for many (cf. Is. 52:13 – 53:12).

When John says that Isaiah 'saw his glory and spoke of him' (John 12:41), does he mean that the prophet saw the glory of the pre-incarnate Christ when he 'saw the Lord sitting upon a throne, high and lifted up' (Is. 6:1)? The quotation from Isaiah 6:10 in the preceding verse certainly takes us back to the context in which the prophet received his commission. However, caution is necessary at this point. John Calvin wisely observed: 'John tells us that it was Christ (John 12:41), and justly, for God never revealed himself to the Fathers but in his eternal Word and only begotten Son. Yet it is wrong, I think, to limit this, as some do, to the person of Christ; for it is *indefinitely*, on the contrary, that the Prophet calls him God.'[11]

When Isaiah saw God as sovereign in human form, he saw the glory that would ultimately be manifested in the incarnation of the Son of God (John 1:14). Alternatively, John may mean that 'Isaiah looked into the future, and saw the life and glory of Jesus.'[12] Isaiah saw this not only in the vision of chapter 6 but in the whole pattern of revelation given to him and recorded in subsequent chapters. The culmination of this revelation of the glory of God is seen in the suffering and glorification of the Servant of the Lord in Isaiah 52:13 – 53:12, to which John's quote in 12:38 draws our attention.

'The way of New Testament references' leads me to consider

---

11. John Calvin, *Isaiah*, Vol. 3 (Grand Rapids, MI: Associated Publishers and Authors), p. 86 (my emphasis). It is interesting to note that, according to Paul in Acts 28:25–26, 'the Holy Spirit' spoke to Israel through the Lord's call to Isaiah. In other words, John and Paul find in Isaiah 6 'that which will accommodate the full revelation of the triune God' (Motyer).

12. R. E. Brown, *The Gospel According to John 1 – 12*, Anchor Bible 29 (Garden City, NY: Doubleday, 1966), p. 487. Cf. D. A. Carson, *The Gospel According to John* (Leicester: Inter-Varsity Press; Grand Rapids, MI: Eerdmans, 1991), pp. 449–450.

Isaiah 6 more broadly in the flow of redemptive history. There is a 'fulfilment' of Isaiah 6 in the person and work of Jesus Christ. The holiness and glory of God which was uniquely revealed to Isaiah is now available for all to see in Christ. He is more than a divinely authorized prophet of the Lord. Only the Son 'who is at the Father's side' has made God truly known (John 1:18). According to his own promise, those who have 'seen the Son', recognizing and responding to him as the incarnate Lord, have 'seen the Father' (14:9). Moreover, Jesus Christ is the king in whose hands has been placed the judgment of all humanity (5:22–24). He is also the one through whom God provides the way of atonement which saves his 'holy seed' for eternity (10:11–18).

So Isaiah 6 points us to the absolute sovereignty of the Lord Jesus Christ and his holiness in judgment and salvation. He rules the universe and holds the destiny of the nations in his hand. He is the one to whom each individual must give account. The stability, peace and prosperity achieved by earthly rulers can disguise the need to relate to him as the true king. Until we have acknowledged Jesus Christ in his awesome power and saving grace, we have not experienced the reality behind everything that exists and behind every event of our lives.

2. The way the true king implements his rule (Is. 6:8–13)

[8]And I heard the voice of the Lord saying, 'Whom shall I send, and who will go for us?' Then I said, 'Here am I! Send me.' [9]And he said, 'Go, and say to this people:

"'Keep on hearing, but do not understand;
    keep on seeing, but do not perceive."
[10]Make the heart of this people dull,
    and their ears heavy,
    and blind their eyes;
lest they see with their eyes,
    and hear with their ears,

and understand with their hearts,
    and turn and be healed.'
[11]Then I said, 'How long, O Lord?'
    And he said:
'Until cities lie waste
    without inhabitant,
and houses without people,
    and the land is a desolate waste,
[12]and the Lord removes people far away,
    and the forsaken places are
        many in the midst of the land.
[13]And though a tenth remain in it,
    it will be burned again,
like a terebinth or an oak,
    whose stump remains
        when it is felled.'
The holy seed is its stump.

a. Sending his servants to proclaim his word

'It now becomes apparent why the "lips" and "mouth" have been so prominent in verses 5–7. The Lord seeks a messenger, and Isaiah, now cleansed, is ready and willing to be his mouthpiece' (Webb). This passage shows us how God achieves his purposes of judgment and salvation through the agency of his word. He implements his rule, not by force of arms or political manipulation, but by the revelation he gives to his servants the prophets (cf. Jer. 1; Ezek. 2; Amos 3:1–8).

The Lord, whom Isaiah saw 'sitting upon a throne, high and lifted up' (Is. 6:1), also dwells with 'him who is of a contrite and lowly spirit, to revive the spirit of the lowly, and to revive the heart of the contrite' (57:15). That was Isaiah's own experience, as he 'heard the voice of the Lord saying, "Whom shall I send, and who will go for us?"' (6:8). God's unique call to Isaiah was in the form of a question, posing a challenge to obedience. The plural 'for us' could be an address to the heavenly host (1 Kgs. 22:19) or a plural of majesty. But it could also indicate that 'in the Speaker Himself there is a plurality of persons' (Young).[13] Isaiah's willing response ('Here am I! Send me.') shows the gracious effect of God's initiative towards him, revealing himself and assuring the prophet of his forgiveness and acceptance.

b. Using his word to harden some

Isaiah's message was to be primarily one of judgment (Is. 6:9–13), both in content and effect. By implication, 'sentence has been passed on the nation in heaven; Isaiah's preaching will put it into effect on earth' (Webb). The prophet's specific calling was to 'Go, and say to this people: "Keep on hearing, but do not understand; keep on seeing, but do not perceive"' (6:9). With such a provocative challenge, he would reveal their spiritual insensitivity and hardness of heart (cf. 1:2–5). Outer faculties ('hearing' / 'seeing') are mentioned, along with inner ones ('understand' / 'perceive'), to emphasize 'a total inability to comprehend' (Motyer).

The Lord would not relieve this situation but would further harden their hearts through the prophet's ministry. God's word produces the outcome it predicts! Isaiah was commanded to 'make the heart of this people dull, and their ears heavy, and blind their eyes; lest they see with their eyes, and hear with their ears, and understand with their hearts, and turn and be healed' (6:10). Once again, the inner and outer faculties are highlighted, this time in a rounded structure ('heart', 'ears', 'eyes', 'eyes', 'ears', 'heart'), to emphasize their spiritual insensitivity. Even though the prophet did preach healing and hope, the effect for so many was still hardening and destruction.

Motyer rightly points out that 'Isaiah did not understand his commission as one to blind people by obscurity of expression or complexity of message.' Indeed, he taught with a simplicity and

---

13. Young sees this as foreshadowing, rather than revealing in its fullness, the doctrine of the Trinity, 'which God graciously revealed in fuller measure to the saints of New Testament times'.

clarity that makes his message relatively easy to understand at an intellectual level. Countless generations of believers have been blessed by his wonderful prophecies of salvation by divine grace. But the Lord was revealing to Isaiah in advance that his people would be unwilling to receive and act upon his message. Humility and repentance would be required – a radical reorientation of life towards God, which they would not accept. The more Isaiah declared God's will, the more they would reject it and harden their hearts. We see the same process operating when God called Moses to challenge Pharaoh about letting the Israelites go from Egypt (Exod. 4:21–23). God's command had to be taken to Pharaoh, even though the Lord indicated that he would harden Pharaoh's heart.[14]

The imperatives of Isaiah 6:9–10 express an inevitable outcome of Isaiah's ministry (cf. 2:9). And we learn from chapters 7 – 11 that this was exactly how things happened. The unresponsiveness of the people, which was their own fault, became an aspect of God's judgment on them. He chose to leave them hardened and even to harden them further by his words of warning through the prophet.

With such a dismal prospect for his ministry ahead of him, Isaiah asks, 'How long, O Lord?' The answer is that he will have to continue preaching, 'Until cities lie waste without inhabitant, and houses without people, and the land is a desolate waste, and the LORD removes people far away, and the forsaken places are many in the midst of the land' (Is. 6:11–12). Cities, houses and land would be emptied, because the population would be deported ('the LORD removes people far away'). This would fulfil the warning given in

---

14. There are nine references to the Lord hardening Pharaoh's heart in Exodus (4:21; 7:3; 9:12; 10:1, 20, 27; 11:10; 14:4, 8) and three to Pharaoh hardening his own heart (8:15, 32; 9:34). God's sovereignty and human responsibility in the process are acknowledged, though there is no explanation of how they work together. Motyer observes that God knows in advance what will happen and appoints this hardening 'as he presides in perfect justice over the psychological process he created'.

Deuteronomy 28:36–68 about the eventual outcome of rebellion against God and his covenant.

Oswalt portrays the situation in this way:

> The land was not theirs to possess as their own. Rather, they possessed it in trust from the true landowner, God. So long as they remained in God's favor, by living lives in keeping with his character, then the land was theirs to develop and to enjoy. But if they ceased to live in obedience to God, the land would vomit them out as it had the Canaanites before them (Lev. 18:25–27).

c. Saving a remnant by his grace

Even in the face of such judgment, a slender hope of salvation is given (Is. 6:13). A remnant of the people will survive by God's grace (cf. 1:9; 10:22). Nevertheless, 'though a tenth remain in it, it will be burned again, like a terebinth or an oak, whose stump remains when it is felled'. Burning implies further punishment or purification of the people. Despite this, the remnant will not be completely destroyed, just as a tree-stump can bring forth new life, even after it is burned by fire.

The last words of God to the prophet are, 'The holy seed is its stump' (lit. 'the seed of holiness its stump'). The term 'seed' (Hebrew *zera'*) suggests regrowth and is later used of the people who will finally enjoy the promises of God.[15] 'Holy' implies that they belong to the Holy One and are dedicated to doing his will (cf. Exod. 19:5–6; Is. 4:2–6). In the predictions of Isaiah 7 – 12, we will see how God's plan of salvation is to be fulfilled through the agency of the Messiah.

Application

God achieves his sovereign purpose, in judgment and salvation, by the word which he gives to his appointed messengers. God's word

---

15. The word is translated 'offspring' in Is. 41:8; 45:25; 53:10; 59:21; 65:9, 23; 66:22.

predicts and brings into effect what he intends. Isaiah was used to expose the unresponsiveness of his contemporaries and to further their hardness of heart as they plunged into greater unbelief and fear. Judgment came through this prophetic activity and the devastation of land and people that followed. But out of this trial and suffering God would preserve a holy remnant, again by his word.

This is what Greidanus calls a 'longitudinal theme' in the Bible. God has always used his word to achieve his purposes of judgment and salvation. In redemptive history, however, Jesus' proclamation of 'the gospel of the kingdom' (Matt. 4:23) or 'the gospel of God' (Mark 1:14–15) was the climax of this process. Accompanied by his mighty works, his word was the way he asserted that God's ultimate purpose for Israel and the nations was being fulfilled ('the kingdom of God is at hand; repent and believe in the gospel'). As he preached this message in various ways, he faced individuals with the implications of God's rule for their lives individually. They could enter into his salvation or remain under judgment.

Jesus' use of Isaiah 6:9–10 to explain the effect of his teaching with parables (Mark 4:11–12; Matt. 13:14–15; Luke 8:10) suggests a special parallel with the commission and experience of Isaiah and a development. Once again we may be guided by 'the way of New Testament references'. Jesus' teaching was not meant to obscure and alienate. But constant exposure to the truth – in word or deed – leaves those who reject it in an even more hardened condition. It exposes and furthers human rebellion against God, until God himself intervenes to soften hearts, and to give understanding and faith. So the unbelieving reception of Jesus by the people of his time is 'the greater fulfilment of God's words to the prophet Isaiah'.[16] The difference in Jesus' situation is that acceptance of his word leads to eternal life and rejection of his word leads to eternal condemnation

---

16. Longenecker, *Biblical Exegesis*, p. 156. We may note a progression from Isaiah to Jesus, inasmuch as the rejection of Jesus and his words excludes people from God's eschatological kingdom.

(e.g. Mark. 8:34–38; 10:23–31). The ministry of Isaiah is a typological anticipation of the eschatological ministry of the Messiah.

Another longitudinal theme highlighted in Isaiah 6:13 is that of the remnant. Even in the course of Jesus' earthly ministry, a holy remnant emerges in those who follow him. They become his disciples by believing his word. The extraordinary outpouring of God's Spirit after Jesus' death, resurrection and ascension made it possible for many more Israelites to become part of that holy remnant (Acts 2:41; 4:4; 6:7). And from their midst, the gospel went out to the Gentiles, so that God began to bless the nations through their testimony to Jesus. But as the story of Acts progresses, we read of considerable opposition to the word of the Lord, quite often from Jewish quarters (e.g. Acts 13:44–50; 17:5–9).

It is significant that in Acts 28:25–28, as Paul experiences opposition from Jews in Rome, he cites Isaiah 6:9–10 against them. The apostle introduces his citation with these words: 'The Holy Spirit was right in saying to your fathers through Isaiah the prophet …' What was revealed to a previous generation by the Holy Spirit was now being manifested in their lives. As Paul proclaimed Christ to them, they appeared to be hardening their hearts in unbelief. His gospel preaching revealed the serious position they were in before God. Paul shared in the fulfilment of Isaiah 6:9–10 because he preached the message of Jesus about the kingdom of God being at hand and offered Jews salvation through Jesus the Messiah.

The same process of exposing unbelief and furthering hardness of heart towards God continues today through the preaching of the gospel. Of course, the gospel is a word of salvation and many find life through believing it. But it is also a word that judges and divides, even as it is proclaimed. Paul found that to be true in his ministry to Jews and Gentiles alike (cf. 1 Cor. 1:18–24). As we share the gospel with friends and neighbours, we must be prepared for the same outcomes. God may use it to bring people to trust in Christ and find life or to harden their hearts in unbelief.

This is difficult teaching for some to accept because it is tied up with the issue of predestination and election. Whatever our concerns are, we must acknowledge that what was true for Isaiah, for Jesus, and for the apostles, must be true for us. God chooses to use his word to achieve his purposes of judgment and salvation. Our task is to be faithful in sharing that word and to pray for the salvation of those with whom we share it.

3 Two Children: Signs of God's Intent
(Isaiah 7)

Children can be a sign of hope. As the survivors of a war, they may represent the possibility of new life for a battered nation. As a new generation in any culture, with a chance to learn from the mistakes of their parents, they may be a sign of better things to come. When God wanted to speak to the king of Judah about his intentions for his people in the eighth century BC, he used two children as part of the message. Isaiah's son is important in the first half of this chapter (7:1–9) and 'the virgin's' son in the second half (7:10–25). One is present, the other is yet to be born. Two more children are introduced in later prophecies (8:1–4; 9:6–7).

The two children in Isaiah 7 point to the fact that God is about to judge his people for their faithlessness and rebellion. But a remnant will be saved and be enabled to return to the Lord. Their salvation will be a sign of God's continuing presence with his people, to bless them and to make them a blessing to the whole world.

The setting

At the end of Uzziah's long reign, a powerful new ruler assumed control in far-off Assyria. His name was Tiglath-pileser III. When he captured the Syrian city of Arpad in 740, cities and states in the region began to fear for their future. Rezin of Damascus, Menahem of Israel (the northern kingdom), Hiram of Tyre and others began to pay tribute to Assyria.[1] However, when Pekah became king over Israel in Samaria (737), he formed an anti-Assyrian coalition with Rezin that was to have disastrous consequences.

The international situation was clearly very threatening when Isaiah began his ministry in Jerusalem. At the same time, Isaiah 1 – 5 reveals a depressing situation in Judah itself: injustice, oppression, religious hypocrisy, idolatry and self-indulgence were rife. Uzziah's son Jotham (740/39–732/31) refused to join the alliance of Pekah and Rezin against Assyria, and so these two kings began to move against Judah (2 Kgs. 15:37). However, Jotham died and the full force of this attack was experienced when his son Ahaz (732/31–716/15) came to the throne of Judah (2 Kgs. 16:1; Is. 7:1). According to Isaiah 7:6, the aim of the northern alliance was to replace Ahaz with 'the son of Tabeel'.

Something of the character of Ahaz and his reign is revealed by the account in 2 Kings 16:2–4:

> Ahaz was twenty years old when he began to reign, and he reigned sixteen years in Jerusalem. And he did not do what was right in the eyes of the Lord his God, as his father David had done, but he walked in the way of the kings of Israel. He even burned his son as an offering, according to the despicable practices of the nations whom the Lord

---

1. Cf. 2 Kgs. 15:19–20, where Pul appears as an abbreviation for Tiglath-pileser. For further information about this period, see a standard history of Israel such as J. Bright, *A History of Israel* (4th ed.; Louisville, KT: Westminster John Knox, 2000).

drove out before the people of Israel. And he sacrificed and made offerings on the high places and on the hills and under every green tree.

With his throne endangered, and fearful that Judah would be overwhelmed by its enemies, Ahaz sent messengers to Tiglath-pileser king of Assyria, saying:

> 'I am your servant and your son. Come up and rescue me from the hand of the king of Syria and from the hand of the king of Israel, who are attacking me.' Ahaz also took the silver and gold that was found in the house of the LORD and in the treasures of the king's house and sent a present to the king of Assyria. And the king of Assyria listened to him. The king of Assyria marched up against Damascus and took it, carrying its people captive to Kir, and he killed Rezin (2 Kgs. 16:7–9).

This was like a mouse asking a cat for help against another mouse, says Oswalt. Only the cat could win! When the Assyrians had deposed Pekah and destroyed Damascus (732), Ahaz was obliged to appear before Tiglath-pileser to express allegiance to him and to his gods. Peace was secured at a terrible price and the temple in Jerusalem was inevitably corrupted by this new allegiance to a pagan king (cf. 2 Kgs. 16:10–18).

Such was the context in which the prophecies of Isaiah 6 – 12 were delivered. These chapters provide an historical introduction to the whole section concluding with chapter 39. King Ahaz and most of the people of Judah failed to trust in God and foolishly relied on Assyria. Trust is a unifying theme not only in Isaiah 6 – 12 but also in the whole first half of the book. Trust in God and its consequences is contrasted with trust in other nations and its consequences. In the final analysis, these issues are presented on a cosmic scale, relating to the end of history and the final accomplishment of God's plans for his creation.

So serious was the situation that Isaiah predicted a terrible outcome for Israel and Judah. But he also insists that nothing will alter God's intention to demonstrate his trustworthiness and saving power. He will fulfil his covenant promises and ultimately bring blessing to the whole world through his chosen king and the people who belong to him.

1. The prophet and his son (Is. 7:1–9)

¹In the days of Ahaz the son of Jotham, son of Uzziah, king of Judah, Rezin the king of Syria and Pekah the son of Remaliah the king of Israel came up to Jerusalem to wage war against it, but could not yet mount an attack against it. ²When the house of David was told, 'Syria is in league with Ephraim,' the heart of Ahaz and the heart of his people shook as the trees of the forest shake before the wind.

³And the LORD said to Isaiah, 'Go out to meet Ahaz, you and Shear-jashub your son, at the end of the conduit of the upper pool on the highway to the Washer's Field. ⁴And say to him, "Be careful, be quiet, do not fear, and do not let your heart be faint because of these two smouldering stumps of firebrands, at the fierce anger of Rezin and Syria and the son of Remaliah. ⁵Because Syria, with Ephraim and the son of Remaliah, has devised evil against you, saying, ⁶'Let us go up against Judah and terrify it, and let us conquer it for ourselves, and set up the son of Tabeel as king in the midst of it,' ⁷thus says the Lord GOD:

'"It shall not stand,
      and it shall not come to pass.
⁸For the head of Syria is Damascus,
      and the head of Damascus is Rezin.

(Within sixty-five years Ephraim will be broken to pieces so that it will no longer be a people.)

⁹'"And the head of Ephraim is Samaria,
      and the head of Samaria is the son of Remaliah.
If you are not firm in faith,
      you will not be firm at all."'

Ahaz and his people were panic-stricken in the face of invasion (Is. 7:1–2). Their opponents were King Rezin of Damascus in Syria and King Pekah of Samaria in Israel/Ephraim. As the living head of 'the house of David', Ahaz king of Judah should have realized his special responsibility to lead the people with confidence in God and his promises. But 'the heart of Ahaz and the heart of his people shook as the trees of the forest shake before the wind'.

Ahaz was investigating Jerusalem's water supply, presumably in preparation for the coming siege, when the prophet met him (7:3). Isaiah was commanded by the Lord to take his son Shear-jashub with him, because of the significance of his name: 'a remnant will turn/return' or 'a remnant will repent'. Arising out of his commissioning experience, Isaiah knew that the approaching judgment of God would leave only a remnant of the people (6:13). He named his child to express that critical message of impending judgment, with the hope of grace and salvation for 'the holy seed'.

The prophet also used a powerful metaphor to show that Ahaz had nothing to fear from the kings of Israel and Syria: 'Be careful, be quiet, do not fear, and do not let your heart be faint because of these two smouldering stumps of firebrands' (7:4). His opponents are likened to the charcoal that is left when a fire goes out! The glory of these two enemies would soon pass away, but the glory and the power of the God of Israel would not. Tiglath-pileser deposed Pekah and destroyed Damascus in 732. Samaria fell to the Assyrians in 721.

Isaiah goes on to reinforce his message with a poetic oracle (7:7–9). This begins with a clear promise concerning the plan to conquer Jerusalem and 'set up the son of Tabeel as king in the midst of it' (v. 5). Very simply, 'says the Lord GOD: It shall not stand, and it shall not come to pass'. The prophet then reminds Ahaz that Rezin was only 'head of Damascus' in Syria and Pekah the son of Remaliah was only 'head of Samaria' in Ephraim – two small fish in the 'big pond' of the Ancient Near East! These 'heads' would soon fall and Ephraim/Israel would soon disappear as a nation ('Within sixty-five years Ephraim will be broken to pieces so that it will no longer be a people').

What is left unsaid, but which should have been understood by Ahaz and his people, is that the head of Judah is Jerusalem and the head of Jerusalem is David's son. According to 2 Samuel 7:14–16, David's son is God's son – by divine appointment. God established a special relationship with the house of David, as a means of fulfilling his covenant promises to Israel. Even though God might punish David's offspring, he would never completely abandon the house of David! Furthermore, according to Isaiah 2:1–4, Jerusalem was significant for the fulfilment of God's plan to bless the whole created order – how could he simply let it go?

The challenge to Ahaz and his people is to believe the promise of God specifically given in Isaiah 7:7 and to trust in God's long-standing commitment to Israel and the Davidic kings. But with the promise comes the warning: 'if you are not firm in faith, you will not be firm at all' (v. 9b). God's purpose will continue and be fulfilled, although Ahaz and his contemporaries may be cast aside because of unbelief. There is no fatalism in Scripture. This passage presents a simple challenge to Ahaz and his generation. Will they experience the blessing of God through faith or will they experience the judgment of God because of unbelief? There is no way of being truly firm or secure in life apart from being firm in faith.

Application

The critical issue of faith in the living God was being played out in Isaiah's time on an international scale. If Ahaz and his people maintained their trust in God, they could experience his deliverance in the present and on into the future. If they failed to trust God and relied on human powers, they would be abandoning God's call to be a distinct and holy people (cf. Exod. 19:5–6), a channel for his truth and blessing for the rest of the world.

The message conveyed by the name of Isaiah's son was a warning, but also an encouragement. God had acted in judgment against the house of David immediately after Solomon's reign, allowing the ten tribes to separate from Judah and Benjamin (1 Kgs. 12:1–24). But the northern kingdom was characterized by idolatry and false religion from the start (1 Kgs. 12:25–33). God would not allow these rebellious tribes to conquer the southern tribes and overturn the Davidic kingship. In fact, he would reduce Israel to a remnant and destroy the kings who were in league against Jerusalem.

But could God be trusted? 'The heart of Ahaz and the heart of his people shook as the trees of the forest shake before the wind', because they saw the strength and determination of their enemies. They could hardly think of God and his promises when their immediate circumstances seemed to be so overwhelming.

Faith in God is such an elementary biblical injunction that we are often tempted to look for more spectacular or impressive solutions to our problems. Trusting in God requires patience and perseverance, when everything around us seems to be signalling disaster and impending failure. However, whether a personal or a national crisis, we never get beyond the requirement for faith, no matter how difficult the situation nor how mature we may be as Christians. Faith is fundamental to a relationship with God because it honours God as God, by taking him at his word and waiting for him to fulfil it.

At this stage in Isaiah's prophecy, there is no call for an articulate faith in the Messiah as the agent of God's salvation. The focus is on 'the Lord God', who made himself known through promises and mighty acts in Israel's past, demonstrating his commitment to them as his covenant people. Nevertheless, the prophet's challenge to Ahaz and his contemporaries should lead Christian readers to trust more firmly in the Lord Jesus Christ. We should respond like that, not simply because of some analogy in our situation, or because faith is a longitudinal theme in the Bible, but because 'the way of redemptive-historical progression' leads us inexorably to Christ and his saving work.

Now that the fulfilment of God's promises has come in Jesus Christ, our security and blessing is tied up with the Son of David, whom God has appointed to be the Saviour of the world (e.g. Rom. 1:1–6; 8:31–39; 16:25–27). No trial can be endured or divine comfort enjoyed apart from him (e.g. 2 Cor. 1:3–11). We cannot be the holy people of God under the New Covenant, a channel for his truth and blessing for the rest of the world, without explicit and continuing faith in Christ. And whatever may come our way, according to the Revelation to John, the victory over all our enemies lies in the hands of the exalted Son of God!

2. The virgin and her son (Is. 7:10–25)

[10]Again the LORD spoke to Ahaz, [11]'Ask a sign of the LORD your God; let it be deep as Sheol or high as heaven.' [12]But Ahaz said, 'I will not ask, and I will not put the LORD to the test.' [13]And he said, 'Hear then, O house of David! Is it too little for you to weary men, that you weary my God also? [14]Therefore the Lord himself will give you a sign. Behold, the virgin shall conceive and bear a son, and shall call his name Immanuel. [15]He shall eat curds and honey when he knows how to refuse the evil and choose the good. [16]For before the boy knows how to refuse the evil and choose the good, the land whose two kings you dread will be deserted. [17]The LORD will bring upon you and upon your people and upon your father's house such days as have not come since the day that Ephraim departed from Judah – the king of Assyria.'

[18]In that day the LORD will whistle for the fly that is at the end of the streams of Egypt, and for the bee that is in the land of Assyria. [19]And they will all come and settle in the steep ravines, and in the clefts of the rocks, and on all the thorn bushes, and on all the pastures.

[20]In that day the LORD will shave with a razor that is hired beyond the River – with the king of Assyria – the head and the hair of the feet, and it will sweep away the beard also.

[21]In that day a man will keep alive a young cow and two sheep, [22]and because of the abundance of milk that they give, he will eat curds, for everyone who is left in the land will eat curds and honey.

[23]In that day every place where there used to be a thousand vines, worth a thousand shekels of silver, will become briers and thorns. [24]With bow and arrows a man will come there, for all the land will be briers and thorns. [25]And as for all the hills that used to be hoed with a hoe, you will

not come there for fear of briers and thorns, but they will become a place where cattle are let loose and where sheep tread.

How will Ahaz be established by the Lord and enabled to 'stand firm in faith' (Is. 7:9b)? God graciously invites him to 'ask a sign' – to test God (vv. 10–11), though it is really Ahaz who is being tested! This is a critical moment in the history of the people of God and in the destiny of the house of David in Jerusalem.

It is unusual in Scripture for the Lord to invite people to seek such a sign, but the magnitude of the offer ('deep as Sheol or high as heaven') highlights the seriousness of the situation. Whatever sign is needed to give Ahaz confidence in God will be granted! Signs cannot create faith, but they are given to inform and strengthen faith. The Bible speaks of miraculous or supernatural events as signs (e.g. Deut. 6:22 [Moses]; John 6:14 [Jesus]). It also identifies certain evidential events which fulfil predictions as divinely given signs (e.g. Is. 8:18 [Isaiah and his 'children']; 1 Sam. 2:34 [the death of Hophni and Phinehas on the same day]; Luke 2:12 [the child in the manger]).

But Ahaz's mind is already made up. He does not want to be assured that trust in God is possible: it could only be an embarrassment to him and expose his unbelief! So he excuses himself on pious grounds, saying, 'I will not ask, and I will not put the LORD to the test.' This appears to be alluding to Deuteronomy 6:16 ('You shall not put the LORD your God to the test, as you tested him at Massah'). Demanding a sign to prove God is certainly forbidden. But asking for a sign when it is offered is no sin (cf. 2 Kgs. 20:8–11; Mal. 3:10; Ps. 34:6).

Ahaz's false piety is condemned because it is an expression of unbelief and rebellion – it 'wearies' God (Is. 7:13). Trying the patience of God is so serious in this situation that the Lord himself freely offers 'a sign' – to condemn 'the house of David' and yet offer a glimmer of hope to believers at the same time: 'Behold, the virgin shall conceive and bear a son, and shall call his name Immanuel' (v. 14).

Great debate has taken place about the precise meaning of this verse. The Hebrew word 'almâ typically means 'a young woman of marriageable age' or 'a maiden'. However, it specifically means 'a virgin' in certain contexts (e.g. Gen. 24:43; Exod. 2:8; Song 6:8) and could easily be rendered that way here. A virginal conception may not be the main emphasis in the passage, but the prophet's choice of words allows for that possibility ('the virgin shall conceive and bear a son'). An ordinary birth would not seem to meet the requirements of the promised 'sign' (Is. 7:11, 14).

'The virgin' appears to be a well-known figure, as the definite article suggests (the prophet does not say 'a virgin'). In Isaiah's vision there is, unusually, no mention of a father in connection with the conception or naming of her child. This certainly expresses something different from the ordinary custom.[2] 'Immanuel' recalls the promises of God's special presence with his covenant people to bless them (e.g. Gen. 28:13–15; Exod. 3:7–8; 19:4). Despite the approaching judgment, the apparently miraculous birth of this child is a sign that God will continue to dwell with his people, to fulfil his purpose for them and through them.

In the canon of Scripture, there is no doubt that this text pre-eminently points to the virgin birth of the Son of God, who is truly 'Immanuel', 'God with us' (cf. Matt. 1:23). Some commentators see Isaiah 7:14 as a direct and uncomplicated revelation of the coming of the Saviour, more than 700 years later. 'In vision Isaiah was allowed to see the virgin, and it is the announcement of what he is permitted to see in vision that he declared unto Ahaz and the nation' (Young). The birth of the virgin's son is the sign that Ahaz has nothing to fear from the

---

2. In the ultimate fulfilment of this prophecy (Matt. 1:18–25), the angel of the Lord instructs Joseph to name the child Jesus ('for he will save his people from their sins'). By exercising the father's right to name the child, he acknowledged Mary's child as his legitimate son. Jesus did not bear 'Immanuel' as an actual name, but it indicates his true character as the one who brings God into the human situation personally.

northern alliance. In the birth of this child, God would be with his people in a new and remarkable way.

However, the sign that is given must have an immediate relevance to the historical context. For example, the deliverance from Syria and Ephraim will occur some little time after the birth of this child. When it is said, 'He shall eat curds and honey when he knows how to refuse the evil and choose the good' (Is. 7:15), the meaning is that when he reaches the years of discretion, he will eat the food of poverty and disaster.[3] Indeed, before he reaches the years of discretion, the collapse of Syria and Ephraim will take place. 'For before the boy knows how to refuse the evil and choose the good, the land whose two kings you dread will be deserted' (v. 16). Then the Assyrians whom God will use to bring about this judgment will turn on Judah and its royal house (v. 17)!

'Immanuel's birth is imminent, and surely Isaiah's hearers would have understood it in this way' (Motyer). So some commentators have argued that the immediate reference is to the birth of king Hezekiah or Isaiah's second son in 8:1–4, but none of these will fit very well, in terms of timing or significance. No other biblical figure such as Moses, Joshua or David is ever given such a name as Immanuel. 'It is a title expressive of some extraordinary excellence and authority which he possesses above others.'[4]

The best option is to see the virgin in the first instance as a figure for 'the daughter Zion' (Is. 1:8; cf. 37:22, 'the virgin daughter of Zion') and to understand her *son* as the faithful remnant who will emerge from her sufferings (Webb).[5] This will be truly a

---

3. Note how 'curds and honey' is defined by the context in vv. 21–22 as a sign of deprivation, not a sign of plenty.

4. Calvin, *Isaiah*, Vol. 3, p. 109. Calvin takes the prophecy as a simple and direct prediction of the birth of the Messiah, but makes a jump in v. 16 from Christ to 'all children', to make sense of the flow of the argument from v. 14. However, this last point seems unwarranted and invalid.

5. The view presented in Webb's commentary is argued more fully in his

miraculous 'birth' in the context of God's impending judgment. The idea that Jerusalem or Zion is a barren woman who gives birth to many children is found in 54:1–8. The idea that she gives birth through the pain of the Babylonian exile occurs in 66:7–9. Prior to 7:14, remnant theology was highlighted in terms of the 'holy seed' (6:13), surviving the fires of judgment. Isaiah's son was named 'a remnant shall return/repent' (7:3). In chapter 8, the title Immanuel really belongs to the small community of believers who gather around the prophet (8:16–18). They are a sign of warning to Ahaz and his people concerning the coming judgment of God, and a sign of hope to those who repent. A remnant will survive by God's grace and be the continuing sign of his presence with his people and his commitment to fulfil his purposes through them.

Isaiah 7 concludes with graphic pictures of the judgment to come, spelling out the implications of v. 17. This is the pain through which the virgin daughter of Zion will give birth to the 'holy seed'. The Lord himself is in charge of the whole process (vv. 18–20). He will 'whistle' for the nations to come and devastate the land. He will use the king of Assyria to 'shave' his people, even 'the beard', taking away their self-respect. The land will be depopulated and those who are left will only be able to 'keep alive a young cow and two sheep' and to 'eat curds and honey' (vv. 21–22). Although this last expression speaks of deprivation, the implication is that God will not leave his people to starve. Tillable land will revert to a wilderness, only fit for hunting (vv. 23–25). So the fruitfulness and joy of Israel's paradise will disappear (cf. Deut. 8:7–10). Those who remain will be like Adam cast out of the Garden of Eden, forced to struggle against 'briers and thorns' to survive (cf. Gen. 3:17–19).

---

article, 'Zion in Transformation: A Literary Approach to Isaiah', in D. J. A. Clines, S. E. Fowl, S. E. Porter (eds.), *The Bible in Three Dimensions* (Sheffield: JSOT, 1990), pp. 65–84 (81–84).

Application

According to the New Testament, Jesus is 'God with us' in a unique and personal way. He is the one who fulfils Israel's destiny by his perfect obedience, who experiences our punishment in his suffering and brings salvation to the nations (cf. Gen. 12:1–3; Gal. 3:7–14). Matthew was right to see the fulfilment of Isaiah 7:14 in Jesus. But this is not the immediate meaning of the verse in its original context. Ahaz was not given a vision of Jesus to trust in at this point but a warning that reliance on Assyria, rather than on the God of the covenant, would bring disaster. With that warning came the amazing promise that the Lord would continue to be with a remnant of his people and would fulfil his saving purpose through them.

As the plan of God unfolds in the next chapters, we read of the divine king emerging from the midst of that remnant (Is. 9:6–7; 11:1–5; cf. Mic. 5:2–4). When we learn that the coming king will be named 'Mighty God, Everlasting Father', we see how God will be with his people in a more personal and direct way than ever before. But at this point in the narrative the hope given concerns the birth of the faithful remnant in whom God's purpose will be realized.

The fundamental challenge of Isaiah 7 is to believe that God can bring salvation out of such terrible judgment; that he can allow such a destructive enemy to flourish and still be gracious; that he can bring a renewed people to birth through terrible pain and judgment, because he is truly *with* his people.

Following Greidanus, we may ask in what sense Isaiah 7:14 was fulfilled, is being fulfilled and will be fulfilled. A remnant of Israel was certainly preserved through the tribulation of the Assyrian attacks and the later captivity in Babylon. Faithful Israelites continued to trust God to fulfil his promises regarding the messianic kingdom. So there was an initial fulfilment of Isaiah's promise in Old Testament times. Then came the definitive and climactic fulfilment in the incarnation of the Son of God (Matt. 1:22–23). The preservation of the remnant in Isaiah's day was an essential part of the process which led to the coming of the Lord

Jesus, the one born literally of a virgin. He emerged from the faithful remnant of Israel (cf. Luke 1 – 2). They received salvation and new life from him, and then became the agents of his salvation and blessing for the whole world (cf. Acts 1 – 8).

But even beyond that, we read of Jesus' promise to be with his followers 'to the end of the age' (Matt. 28:20). This was realized in the sending of the Holy Spirit at Pentecost (Acts 2:33, 38–39). Moreover, God makes those who are part of the true remnant in Jesus Christ themselves a sign to all the world of his saving purposes. Because of Jesus, through the Holy Spirit, God is truly *with us*. Furthermore, the promise of 'God with us' stretches 'even beyond the church age to the new creation when, according to the voice John heard, "the home of God is among mortals. He will dwell with them; they will be his peoples, and God himself will be with them" (Rev. 21:3).'[6]

So there are different levels of fulfilment or application of the 'God with us' theme in Scripture, culminating in the assurance of life for ever in his presence. Immanuel incarnate makes this blessing possible by means of his saving work, and he sustains those who trust in him by his Spirit until they come to the consummation of his plan for them in the new creation.

---

6. Greidanus, *Preaching Christ*, p. 243.

4   Misdirected Fear
(Isaiah 8)

The church in the Western world is in danger of being swamped by secularism and put out of business in some places. One of the reasons for this is a fear on the part of many church leaders of being irrelevant to the contemporary culture. Consequently, the message of Scripture is watered down so that it becomes inoffensive, compromise over moral issues is rife, and church agendas are planned so that the world can approve what we do. The problem with this approach is that unbelievers say, 'Great! You basically think the same way that we do. But we don't have to come and join you because you don't have to be a Christian to be kind, and socially aware, and politically committed!'

In other parts of the world, Christians are afraid of being attacked by Islamic fundamentalists or prevented from sharing their faith by the governing authorities. Loss of life or livelihood is much more terrifying than being thought irrelevant to the surrounding culture! But it is easy to see how compromise or watering down the message is the easiest alternative in both contexts.

Fear of opponents has always been the alternative to a genuine fear of God. We see it in Isaiah's time, in Jesus' time, in the early church and in every era since. If we want to please God and grow the church in a hostile or cynical culture, Isaiah's message to his contemporaries has something important to teach us about fearing God and trusting him to work out his revealed purposes. The key verses in this chapter are:

'Do not call conspiracy all that this people calls conspiracy, and do not fear what they fear, nor be in dread. But the Lord of hosts, him you shall regard as holy. Let him be your fear, and let him be your dread' (Is. 8:12–13).

Isaiah 8 is made up of three oracles, in which Isaiah delivers messages given to him directly from the Lord (vv. 1–4, 5–10, 11–15), followed by a fourth section in which the prophet reflects on the significance of these oracles (vv. 16–22).[1] Thematically, the first two oracles belong together and so I will divide the chapter in a threefold way (vv. 1–10, 11–15, 16–22) to bring out the essential warnings it contains.

1. Beware the overwhelming flood (Is. 8:1–10)

¹Then the LORD said to me, 'Take a large tablet and write on it in common characters, "Belonging to Maher-shalal-hashbaz." ²And I will get reliable witnesses, Uriah the priest and Zechariah the son of Jeberechiah, to attest for me.'

³And I went to the prophetess, and she conceived and bore a son. Then the LORD said to me, 'Call his name Maher-shalal-hashbaz; ⁴for before the boy knows how to cry "My father" or "My mother," the

---

1. Webb notes that the pattern continues in 9:1–7, with a second reflection in 9:1 and a fourth oracle in 9:2–7. Thus, the whole unit extends from 8:1 to 9:7. For the purpose of exposition, however, there is sufficient in Isaiah 8 for one message, and 9:1–7 has a different thrust.

wealth of Damascus and the spoil of Samaria will be carried away before the king of Assyria.'

[5]The LORD spoke to me again: [6]'Because this people have refused the waters of Shiloah that flow gently, and rejoice over Rezin and the son of Remaliah, [7]therefore, behold, the Lord is bringing up against them the waters of the River, mighty and many, the king of Assyria and all his glory. And it will rise over all its channels and go over all its banks, [8]and it will sweep on into Judah, it will overflow and pass on, reaching even to the neck, and its outspread wings will fill the breadth of your land, O Immanuel.'

[9]Be broken, you peoples, and be shattered;
    give ear, all you far countries;
  strap on your armour and be shattered;
    strap on your armour and be shattered.
[10]Take counsel together, but it will come to nothing;
    speak a word, but it will not stand,
    for God is with us.

The opening section of Isaiah 8 is reminiscent of 7:14–17, but this child is clearly different. His mother is not a virgin (the prophet's wife has already given birth to Shear-jashub, mentioned in 7:3). His birth is not announced in a cryptic way to the king, but in an open way for all the people of Judah to see and to hear (8:1–2). The name given (lit. 'the spoil speeds', 'the prey hastens') is a simple warning of imminent judgment (vv. 3–4), rather than an assurance of God's presence to bless and to judge (as with the name 'Immanuel').[2] Though the destruction of Damascus and Samaria signals immediate relief for Judah, the Assyrians will pour down like a mighty river and eventually overwhelm the southern kingdom as well (vv. 5–8)!

---

2. As noted in the previous chapter, the name 'Immanuel' brings the hope of God's presence to save and to bless a remnant, but implies judgment on Ahaz and his apostate nation at the same time.

However, God will not allow this terrifying enemy to make a complete end of his people or their land (vv. 9–10).

Writing the child's name on 'a large tablet', using 'common characters', means advertising the name and its significance well before the birth (v. 1).[3] The summoning of 'reliable witnesses' (v. 2) to this pre-publication of the name is designed to prove that, when the child is finally born and named, he is truly a sign from the Lord. People will not be able to accuse Isaiah of 'prophecy after the fact' (Oswalt). 'Maher-shalal-hashbaz' will become an immediate time indicator of the approaching destruction of the northern alliance threatening Judah (vv. 3–4). For, 'before the boy knows how to cry "My father" or "My mother," the wealth of Damascus and the spoil of Samaria will be carried away before the king of Assyria.' This happened in 732 BC.

Like Ahaz in Isaiah 7, the people are being given a last chance to abandon their faithless scheming and rely entirely on the Lord. 'Maher-shalal-hashbaz' is a sign of judgment on Syria and the northern kingdom of Israel – not yet on Judah. It invites trust in the Lord in response to this promise of deliverance – not complacency or fear.

The next oracle (8:5–10) is about the way the people of Judah reacted to this challenge and how God responded to their unbelief. Some time seems to have elapsed since the birth of Maher-shalal-hashbaz. With unforgettable imagery, the prophet pictures them refusing 'the waters of Shiloah that flow gently' (v. 6). God's help is portrayed in terms of the gentle stream that flows from the Gihon spring to supply water to the lower end of the city of David. At the same time, they seem to have rejoiced at the discomfort of their enemies (they 'rejoice over Rezin and the son of Remaliah') –

---

3. NIV 'with an ordinary pen' is a more literal rendering of the Hebrew. ESV 'in common characters' assumes that the expression is a figure of speech for the script produced by an ordinary stylus, which could be easily read (so also NRSV).

presumably as the events unfolded.[4] There appears to be no fear of God in this response or any recognition of his sovereignty in their deliverance from these enemies. They simply rejoiced in the might of one human power over another, as we so often do, leaving God out of the picture.

Isaiah therefore predicts that the same ally they trusted to defeat their enemies would soon defeat them too. The Lord will send upon them 'the waters of the River, mighty and many', symbolizing 'the king of Assyria and all his glory' (v. 7). Such imagery is very powerful in contrast with 'the waters of Shiloah that flow gently'. The river which represents the king of Assyria and his armies 'will rise over all its channels and go over all its banks, and it will sweep on into Judah' (v. 8).

Despite the seriousness of the warning, however, Isaiah's prediction contains a note of hope and grace. This river will 'overflow and pass on, reaching even to the neck, and its outspread wings will fill the breadth of your land, O Immanuel'. God will not let Judah be totally obliterated: the flood waters will only reach 'the neck', suggesting again that a remnant will be saved. This outcome is also implied by the reference to 'Immanuel'.

'Immanuel' here most obviously refers to the people who are the sign of God's presence – the faithful remnant, kept by the power and grace of God. If 'Immanuel' is taken as referring to an individual in 7:14, it must also be so here. But the third use of this term in 8:14, leading into a series of challenges about seeking refuge in the Lord of hosts and being distinct from the mass of the people (8:15–22), suggests that remnant theology is the controlling idea in the chapter.

The land may be swamped or, changing the metaphor, the people may be overshadowed by their enemy, like a bird with its 'outspread wings'. But those whom God rescues from judgment

---

4. Instead of 'rejoice over' (ESV, NIV), NRSV has 'melt in fear before'. This emendation of the Hebrew is less likely than the more literal rendering of ESV and NIV.

still have a destiny and a role to fulfil in his plan for the world. According to 8:9–10, no matter what the nations throw at God's people, God's purpose will not ultimately be frustrated. Even though they strap on their armour to shatter Israel, they will 'be shattered'. Even though they 'take counsel together', it will 'come to nothing', and what they speak against God's people 'will not stand, for God is with us' (the truth behind the name 'Immanuel' is literally expressed in v. 10).

Application

Following 'the way of analogy' noted by Greidanus, we may observe from this passage both continuity and progression in God's dealings with Israel and, through Christ, with the church. The way of faith in God is represented by Jerusalem and its water supply. The Gihon spring was very vulnerable under enemy attack, but it was God's gift to Jerusalem, to preserve the city and maintain its life. Believers who know that God can be trusted will choose this way, despite its apparent weakness. To choose the way of the world may seem safer (in Judah's case relying on Assyria). But you get what you choose: the world full and plenty, represented by the overflowing Euphrates. This can lead to drowning and death!

Such a warning could be applied to individuals and to churches in our day. Jesus Christ is the source of 'living water', which becomes for believers 'a spring of water welling up to eternal life' (John 4:13–14; 7:37–39). The world can offer nothing like the security and fulfilment found in Christ. But the seductive power and attractiveness of the world continues to confront us, even in our churches. The New Testament challenges us to maintain our confidence in the Lord Jesus and his work for us, rather than trust in human authorities and the wisdom of the world (e.g. 1 Cor. 1:10–31) or human traditions and religious practices (e.g. Col. 2:6–23). We are warned about a friendship with the world which makes one an enemy of God (Jas. 4:1–4). Those who love the world or the things in it will pass away with the world (1 John 2:15–17).

Indeed, there are churches in danger of losing their identity and their very existence because of compromise with the world and its values (Rev. 2 – 3).

Yet God will not leave himself entirely without witnesses, even when the world overwhelms the church at different times and in different places. Isaiah's promise is that the enemy of God's people ultimately will not succeed, 'for God is with us'. Christians are similarly assured that the one who is Immanuel incarnate has ascended into heaven and has poured out his Spirit on his people (Acts 2:33). And he continues to be with his people 'always, to the end of the age' (Matt. 28:20). He will preserve his elect through every trial and challenge (Rom. 8:31–39) and bring them safely to their heavenly inheritance (1 Pet. 1:3–5), which is truly Immanuel's land.

But the challenge of the passage is this: will we prove ourselves to be truly his by constantly looking to him as the life-giving stream of salvation? Will we look instead to the world's power and resources or resort to alternative spiritual powers? Will we panic when disaster comes? Will we follow the crowd or stand firm with the few?

2. Beware the stumbling-stone (Is. 8:11–15)

[11]For the LORD spoke thus to me with his strong hand upon me, and warned me not to walk in the way of this people, saying: [12]'Do not call conspiracy all that this people calls conspiracy, and do not fear what they fear, nor be in dread. [13]But the LORD of hosts, him you shall regard as holy. Let him be your fear, and let him be your dread. [14]And he will become a sanctuary and a stone of offence and a rock of stumbling to both houses of Israel, a trap and a snare to the inhabitants of Jerusalem. [15]And many shall stumble on it. They shall fall and be broken; they shall be snared and taken.'

The broad connection between this oracle and the previous one is clear: the schemes of the nations will not succeed against those who genuinely fear the Lord. It presents the central challenge of the chapter to fear God rather than what others fear.

Isaiah first recalls how powerfully this message was impressed on his consciousness by God ('For the LORD spoke thus to me with his strong hand upon me', 8:11). 'The hand symbolizes personal agency and power (cf. Exod. 6:1)' (Motyer). An intense and direct experience of inspiration is implied (cf. Ezek. 1:3; 3:14). It was a warning for the prophet personally 'not to walk in the way of this people' – not to succumb to their faithlessness. However, the warning was not for the prophet alone, because the commands in 8:12–13 are in the plural. Through the prophet, one group of people in Judah was being warned about adopting the attitude of the other. The faithful are challenged to step out from the crowd and identify with the prophet by not following the way of the majority ('the way of this people').

Negatively, the warning is, 'Do not call conspiracy all that this people calls conspiracy, and do not fear what they fear, nor be in dread' (8:12). 'Conspiracy' here may refer to Isaiah's call for dependence on the Lord rather than on foreign powers. Such a demand seemed to undermine the safety and security of Judah. Those who could think of securing the future only by submitting to Assyria regarded this as treason (Young). Other commentators see 'conspiracy' as a more general reference to 'human machinations' or 'paranoia' in that political situation (Oswalt). But the 'fear' and 'dread' of the people are not so difficult to define. They were afraid of being defeated by Syria and Ephraim, with consequent loss of property, wealth, independence and life. This fear led them to trust the greater political might of Assyria, without realizing that this was like jumping out of the frying pan into the fire!

Positively, the challenge is, 'but the Lord of hosts, him you shall regard as holy. Let him be your fear, and let him be your dread.' The words 'him you shall regard as holy' (lit. 'him you shall sanctify') put everything in perspective. A genuine fear or respect for the Lord arises from treating him as holy and distinct – different from the gods of human imagination and different from human beings in his thoughts and ways (cf. Exod. 15:11–12; Is. 6:1–13; 55:8–9). Isaiah's own experience of the Lord 'high and lifted up' (6:1), utterly holy and his glory filling the whole earth (6:3), was clearly determinative for his life and ministry. In a sense, he is challenging others to share this vision and its implications.

To 'sanctify' God is to acknowledge that he has the right to direct and rule us because of who he is. He is sovereign over all the events of history and over every human authority or supernatural power. 'To fail to sanctify him is to make him appear helpless, indifferent, and unimportant' (Oswalt).[5] God's own self-revelation in Scripture should motivate us to trust him rather than the individuals and forces that seek to oppose him.

To those who truly sanctify him, he becomes 'a sanctuary' (8:14a) – a place of refuge and safety in any storm.[6] There is a play on words in the Hebrew here which is brought out by translating the text more literally: 'him you shall sanctify ... and he will become a sanctuary'. Paradoxically, God offers to become 'a sanctuary' for those who trust him by protecting them from his own judgment against them (expressed in the coming of the Assyrians, 8:7; 10:5–6). The Lord alone will provide salvation, even though chaos, destruction and persecution may be all that appears on the horizon.

To those who do not sanctify him, however, he will be 'a stone of offence and a rock of stumbling to both houses of Israel, a trap and a snare to the inhabitants of Jerusalem' (8:14b). Isaiah is comprehensive in his description of who may stumble over this stone or be trapped and snared by it. 'Both houses of Israel' are

---

5. To fail to sanctify God is to 'profane his holy name' by not treating him appropriately as the Holy One. Cf. Lev. 22:31–33; Num. 20:12; Ezek. 36:20–23; Amos 2:7.

6. The word 'sanctuary' (Hebrew *miqdāš*, 'holy place') is used in connection with the tabernacle (Exod. 25:8) and the temple (1 Chr. 22:19). It was the place where God's people could meet with him and seek his protection (cf. Exod. 21:12–14; Ps. 27:5). The verb 'to sanctify' is *qāḏaš*.

identified, but 'the inhabitants of Jerusalem' are singled out for special mention. Then the prophet broadens out his warning again to say, 'And many shall stumble on it. They shall fall and be broken; they shall be snared and taken.' His warning is as emphatic as it can be!

Here is a great surprise: God himself can be the most difficult 'stumbling-block' that anyone can encounter! The inhabitants of Judah doubtless thought that the northern alliance was the greatest threat to their happiness and security. In due course, they would experience Assyria as 'a trap and a snare'. Isaiah's point is that God can be experienced either as 'sanctuary' or 'stone of offence'.

Those who acknowledge him as the Holy One and submit their lives to his control, discover that they have been drawn by his grace into a relationship that brings peace and security. Those who will not make a place for him in their lives find that they are continually colliding with him, until they come to the point of falling and being broken, only to experience utter destruction.

Application

These verses are applied very deliberately to the Lord Jesus Christ and his people in the New Testament. The Christological significance of the passage in Isaiah is therefore rightfully discerned by what Greidanus terms 'the way of New Testament references'. Key verses from the New Testament lead us into the broad typological structure of the biblical revelation and show us how Isaiah's words are fulfilled in Christ.

In 1 Peter 3:14-15, in the face of persecution (even suffering for what is right), believers are warned, 'Have no fear of them, nor be troubled, but in your hearts regard Christ the Lord as holy'. The first exhortation could be better translated, 'Do not fear what they fear' (NRSV, NIV), which would be closer in sense to Isaiah 8:12. Christians under attack are not to fear what their opponents fear, whether that means fear of false gods or fear of persecution, pain and even death. In this respect their situation is exactly the same as that of believers in Isaiah's time.

The remarkable difference for Peter is that Jesus Christ explicitly replaces 'the Lord of hosts' in Isaiah's challenge. He is the one to sanctify or regard as holy because he is the one whom God has provided to be the ultimate 'sanctuary' for his people under the New Covenant. In Peter's letter, Jesus is the one who ransoms from sin through his death (1 Pet. 1:18–21) and was raised to life to establish an eternal inheritance for us (1 Pet. 1:3–5). But Jesus is also specifically in the New Testament 'a stone of offence and a rock of stumbling' for those who will not trust in him.

Jesus applies a related text from Psalm 118:22–23 to himself in Matthew 21:42–44:

'The stone that the builders rejected
　　has become the cornerstone;
this was the Lord's doing,
　　and it is marvellous in our eyes.'

He then goes on to say to his opponents:

'Therefore I tell you, the kingdom of God will be taken away from you and given to a people producing its fruits. And the one who falls on this stone will be broken to pieces; and when it falls on anyone, it will crush him.'

The last sentence echoes the warning of Isaiah 8:14–15 (cf. Is. 28:16). Jesus the Messiah is not only the precious 'cornerstone' of the new spiritual temple that God is building (Eph. 2:19–22), but he is also the one over whom people trip and fall. The terrible judgment which Isaiah predicted in his day for those who rejected God as 'sanctuary' is now applied to those who reject Jesus as Saviour and Lord.

Following the lead of his master, Peter put several Old Testament 'stone' texts together in 1 Peter 2:6–8, to show that the double-edged nature of God's self-revelation now confronts us specifically in the Lord Jesus. It is in coming to Jesus as 'a living stone' that we can be 'built up as a spiritual house' – a dwelling-place for God by the Spirit (Eph. 2:22). It is in rejecting Jesus that Isaiah's warning comes to its ultimate fulfilment. Those who stumble over this 'stone' are rejected by God for eternity: 'They stumble because they disobey the word, as they were destined to do' (1 Pet. 2:8b; cf. Luke 2:34; Rom. 9:33).

3. Beware the darkness of superstition (Is. 8:16–22)

[16]Bind up the testimony; seal the teaching among my disciples. [17]I will wait for the LORD, who is hiding his face from the house of Jacob, and I will hope in him. [18]Behold, I and the children whom the LORD has given me are signs and portents in Israel from the LORD of hosts, who dwells on Mount Zion. [19]And when they say to you, 'Enquire of the mediums and the necromancers who chirp and mutter,' should not a people enquire of their God? Should they enquire of the dead on behalf of the living? [20]To the teaching and to the testimony! If they will not speak according to this word, it is because they have no dawn. [21]They will pass through the land, greatly distressed and hungry. And when they are hungry, they will be enraged and will speak contemptuously against their king and their God, and turn their faces upward. [22]And they will look to the earth, but behold, distress and darkness, the gloom of anguish. And they will be thrust into thick darkness.

This passage continues to develop the idea that there is a profound division 'between the faithful and the unfaithful within the visible community of God's people, between those who respond to the word of God with obedient faith and those who do not, between the true and the false' (Webb). On the one hand, those who choose to sanctify God will be one with the prophet and his 'children' and will have light and hope. On the other hand, those who refuse to sanctify God will be driven to magic and the occult and thus into deeper darkness and despair.

The imperatives in 8:16 ('Bind up the testimony; seal the teaching among my disciples') suggest the securing of Isaiah's message from tampering and addition, committing it to the care of his disciples.[7] When the prophet speaks about his own trustful waiting upon God ('I will wait for the LORD, who is hiding his face from the house of Jacob, and I will hope in him', v. 17), he appears to be encouraging others to follow his example. His disciples must base their confidence on 'the testimony' and 'the teaching' he has given them, just as he himself does.

Isaiah is also encouraged to 'wait for the LORD' and 'hope in him' because of 'the children whom the LORD has given me' (v. 18). Rather than being his disciples, these 'children' are more obviously the sons with special names, given to make them 'signs and portents in Israel from the LORD of hosts' (cf. 7:3; 8:1–3). His sons were a testimony to the continuing presence and power of 'the LORD of hosts, who dwells on Mount Zion'. Yet Isaiah and his family are effectively the nucleus of the faithful remnant, with others identifying themselves as part of this group by a faithful response to his preaching.

The alternative to being part of the faithful remnant is not religious neutrality or indifference, but the pursuit of 'the mediums and the necromancers who chirp and mutter' (8:19) – superstition and popular religion. Isaiah draws attention to the foolishness of the people who claim to belong to God but do not 'enquire of their God'. And how ridiculous to use mediums 'to enquire of the dead on behalf of the living'! Loss of faith in God and the reliability of his revelation in Scripture opens people to every kind of superstitious nonsense. Hence the prophet's challenge, to resort to 'the teaching and to the testimony!' (v. 20). Mediums and necromancers 'will not speak according to this word', because they prefer the vanity of their own supposed contact with the dead, rather than

---

7. Less likely is Young's suggestion that God commands Isaiah to close the message 'spiritually in the hearts of his disciples' and to leave it there. Oswalt suggests that 'an act of affirmation and attestation' in connection with the prophet's own oracles may be meant.

seeking after the living God. They operate this way because they themselves 'have no dawn'.

This last comment introduces the note of darkness and gloom which concludes the chapter. In Isaiah's vision, those who succumb to superstition and false religion 'will pass through the land, greatly distressed and hungry' (v. 21). Their decision to abandon confidence in God and the light of his revelation will lead to darkness, emptiness and despair. When this happens, 'they will be enraged and will speak contemptuously against their king and their God' (v. 21). Having turned 'their faces upward' and found no help in God, they will 'look to the earth', only to see 'distress and darkness, the gloom of anguish' (v. 22). Isaiah's final comment is that 'they will be thrust into thick darkness'. 'They had loved darkness ... and divine justice has given them what they loved: darkness all around and a dark future ahead, the nemesis of abandoning their God and of refusing his testimony and law' (Motyer).

Application

In times of crisis, people want explanations and they want something of the comfort that religion can bring. But they so often want these things on their own terms – apart from the revelation that comes to us through God's prophets and apostles. Isaiah's challenge to his contemporaries was to join him in trusting the Lord, waiting for him to act according to his own promises. Isaiah's warning was that those who refused to trust God in this way would become more and more fearful, more and more unstable, more and more subject to the powers of darkness. True believers unite around the word of God and draw their strength from that.

How distressing it is to see intelligent people in our own time consulting astrologers and mediums, following New Age philosophies and strange practices, while rejecting God's revealed word. For such people there is 'no dawn' (8:20), but only spiritual darkness. Our task is to demonstrate the futility of seeking an explanation of reality apart from God our Creator and Redeemer, and to be 'signs and portents' ourselves of that revelation. We can do that by maintaining our own confidence in Christ and his promises, while showing the fruit of that faith in our lifestyle (cf. Matt. 5:14–16; 1 Pet. 3:15–16).

But what are the specifically Christological implications of this passage? Once again, New Testament application of key verses gives us the solution. In a passage outlining the special relationship between Christ and his people, Hebrews 2:13 adapts a portion of Isaiah 8:17 and part of 8:18. Applied to Jesus, the words 'I will put my trust in him' mean that Isaiah was a type of the Messiah, having to trust God to fulfil his purposes in the face of opposition and rejection, darkness and death. The faithfulness of Christ, even to death on a cross, not only achieves our eternal salvation (Heb. 5:8–9; 10:10, 14), but also offers the greatest encouragement to persevere to the end in faith ourselves (Heb. 3:1–2; 12:1–3).

From Isaiah 8:18 we see that Isaiah and his children are a type of Christ and his church. The union between Christ and his people originates in the electing grace of the Father ('the children God has given me') and is realized historically by the incarnation and redemptive suffering of the Son of God (Heb. 2:11–18). The reference to Isaiah 8:17 shows how the Father's purpose is fulfilled and realized through the saving action of the Son ('I will put my trust in him'). 'Jesus is now the representative head of a new humanity which is being led to glory through suffering.'[8] The remnant before and after Christ are saved by his unique and perfect sacrificial action (cf. Heb. 9:15) and by persevering in the faith that he makes possible (Heb. 12:1–2).

---

8. W. L. Lane, *Hebrews 1 – 8*, Word Bible Commentary, Vol. 47a (Word: Dallas, 1991), p. 60.

5 The Trustworthiness of God
(Isaiah 9:1–7)

One of the most amazing things about God in Scripture is the fact that he is never frustrated by human sin and never gives up his plans for our good. When *we* are frustrated in some endeavour, we often make radical changes and start on a different track. But not so the God of the Bible. For example, after the fall in Genesis 3, when the offspring of Adam and Eve continue to reject him in all sorts of ways, God acts in judgment but continues to engage with rebellious humanity for their salvation (Gen. 4 – 9). After the tower of Babel incident in Genesis 11, he seeks to establish a new humanity in Abraham who will recognize and serve him (Gen. 12 – 17).

Moving on to Isaiah 7 – 8, we read of the terrible judgment coming upon the people of God in the eighth century BC because of their unfaithfulness. The northern kingdom is to be wiped out by the Assyrian invasion and the southern kingdom decimated. But God will not give up on his people entirely. A remnant will be saved and become the nucleus of a renewed Israel. The remnant represents the truth of God's continuing presence to bless them (hence the name 'Immanuel').

In these chapters we also read of the judgment coming upon the house of David. Poor leadership from the Davidic kings has contributed to the collapse of the nation, politically and spiritually. But Isaiah 9:1–7 makes it clear that God will not even give up on the house of David. He will not be frustrated in his promise to bless his people through David's offspring (2 Sam. 7:12–16). Isaiah 7 – 9 is therefore all about the trustworthiness of God and how his people can continue to rely on him, even through the darkest circumstances. Indeed, at each new stage in the unfolding of God's plan we discover more of his ultimate intentions and how they are fulfilled for us in the Lord Jesus Christ.

Isaiah 9:6–7 is the most explicit messianic promise so far in the book of Isaiah, with its reference to a son who will sit on David's throne and whose kingdom of justice and peace will last for ever. This wonderful prediction is prefaced by two promises relating to the immediate historical context addressed by the prophet. God's light will shine on those who walk in the darkness portrayed at the end of the last chapter (9:1–2; cf. 8:19–22), and God will defeat the enemy he intends to use to punish his rebellious people (9:3–5; cf. 8:5–10).

1. The God who brings light out of darkness (Is. 9:1–2)

¹But there will be no gloom for her who was in anguish. In the former time he brought into contempt the land of Zebulun and the land of Naphtali, but in the latter time he has made glorious the way of the sea, the land beyond the Jordan, Galilee of the nations.

²The people who walked in darkness
    have seen a great light;
those who dwelt in a land of deep darkness,
    on them has light shined.

Isaiah looks into the future and envisages light coming into Israel's 'gloom' and 'anguish'. Bringing light out of darkness is God's role as Creator in Genesis 1. A 'new creation' motif is being suggested here – such a transformation of Israel's situation that only God the Creator can manage it!

The prophet speaks about future events as if they were established already. From his standpoint, even 'the former time' is yet to come, with 'the latter time' emerging beyond that. But he speaks of coming events with the certainty of completed actions. In 'the former time', he will bring 'into contempt the land of Zebulun and the land of Naphtali' (Is. 9:1). In 'the latter time', he will make this region 'glorious'.

This first oracle is particularly significant in its context because Isaiah 8 ends with a desperate picture of people stumbling further and further into darkness and chaos – the result of rejecting the revelation given by God through his prophets (8:16–22, esp. vv. 21–22). It is the darkness of superstition that follows the rejection of the knowledge of God and his will. Such darkness will envelop every area of Israel's life and bring 'gloom' and 'anguish'. Isaiah's promise is specifically for 'the people who walked in darkness ... who dwelt in a land of deep darkness' (9:2).

The wording of 9:1 is amazing because the light appears to dawn first in 'the land of Zebulun and the land of Naphtali', the very area around the Sea of Galilee which would first feel the lash of Assyria! With the coming invasion, God would bring this area 'into contempt'. But where the judgment begins ('in the former time') is where the light and salvation for a new era begins ('in the latter time')! The coming of God's light will make 'glorious the way of the sea, the land beyond the Jordan, Galilee of the nations'. This suggests some extraordinary manifestation of God's glory in that region. Only God can bring transforming light out of such terrible darkness. 'There is light for these people because their sin and rebellion are not enough to keep God from manifesting himself to them' (Oswalt).

Application

Although this prophecy is immediately directed to those portrayed in Isaiah 8:19–22, the promise is capable of a wider application. Darkness and light are important themes running throughout Scripture. Darkness is associated with confusion, deception and divine judgment (e.g. Job 12:20–25; Matt. 8:12; 25:30; John 3:19–20; 9:39–41). Light is associated with salvation and peace (e.g. Ps. 27:1; Luke 1:77–79), truth and life (e.g. Ps. 36:9; John 1:4; 3:21; 8:12). To be in the darkness is to be separated from God, but to be in the light is to be in fellowship with God who is light (1 John 1:5–7). The ultimate manifestation of divine light is in the person and work of the Son of God (e.g. John 8:12; 9:5).

Matthew 4:12–17 quotes Isaiah 9:1–2 and draws attention to the specific fulfilment of this prophecy in Jesus' withdrawal to Galilee and the beginning of his public ministry there.[1] As the prophet looks beyond the immediate judgement of the Assyrian invasion to 'the latter time', he gives his contemporaries a vision of what God will do through the sending of the deliverer who is described in Isaiah 9:6. From the New Testament we know that this is none other than Jesus the Messiah, who is uniquely the Son of God. The messianic light first shone brilliantly in 'Galilee of the nations', foreshadowing Jesus' own commission to take the light of his gospel to all nations (Matt. 28:19).

Here we have a wonderful example of what is called 'a prophetic foreshortening of the future'. Nothing happened between Isaiah's time and the coming of Jesus that could seriously be described as a fulfilment of this promise. The true and ultimate salvation of Israel came roughly 700 years later with Jesus! Isaiah's long-range prophecy

---

1. Matthew's text form is either an independent translation of the Hebrew or else a modification of divergent Greek manuscripts of the OT text, hence the variations in the English. Cf. D. A. Carson, 'Matthew', in F. E. Gaebelein (ed.), *The Expositor's Bible Commentary*, Vol. 8 (Grand Rapids, MI: Zondervan, 1984), pp. 117–118.

was meant to give meaning, purpose and direction to the lives of those who first received it and to every subsequent generation until Jesus appeared in Galilee. They did not need to know God's precise timing of this event for it to give them genuine hope and salvation through Christ (cf. Heb. 9:15).

Isaiah 9:1–2 invites confidence in God's ability to bring us 'the light of life' through the one sent to be 'the light of the world' (John 8:12; 9:5). When people live in the darkness of oppression, false religion or self-indulgence, they normally cannot imagine any possibility of transformation and change. Only the word of God can bring such hope, as it points them to Christ and invites them to open their lives to the light that brings true life. As Christians, we are challenged to behave as those who belong to the light, awaiting the day of Christ's return, when his glory will be fully revealed (cf. Rom. 13:11–14; 1 Thess. 5:4–11).

2. The God who saves his people from oppression and defeat (Is. 9:3–5)

> [3]You have multiplied the nation;
>> you have increased its joy;
> they rejoice before you
>> as with joy at the harvest,
>> as they are glad when they divide the spoil.
> [4]For the yoke of his burden,
>> and the staff for his shoulder,
>> the rod of his oppressor,
>> you have broken as on the day of Midian.
> [5]For every boot of the tramping
>>> warrior in battle tumult
>> and every garment rolled in blood
>> will be burned as fuel for the fire.

The coming of God's glorious light is linked to the bringing of new life to his people. Two promises are first given and then explained.

'You have multiplied the nation' (Is. 9:3) predicts the restoration of Israel after the decimation of the Assyrian invasion. The language suggests the fulfilment of God's original promise to make Abraham's offspring a great nation (Gen. 12:1–3). 'You have increased its joy' (Is. 9:3) is clearly related to this restoration and is likened to 'joy at the harvest' and the exultation of those who 'divide the spoil' after a military victory. God will bring joy into the predicted situation of war and destruction by defeating the enemies of his people.

Like a hymn of praise to God, each of the following verses beginning with the word 'for' spells out more precisely the cause of this joy. Removal of oppressive rule by foreigners is mentioned first (Is. 9:4). God will break the yoke of Israel's burden, 'and the staff for his shoulder, the rod of his oppressor'. Reference to 'the day of Midian' recalls the great deliverance by God which Gideon and his people witnessed in Judges 6 – 7. The coming victory will be similarly miraculous and a sign of God's special care for Israel.

Removal of war itself is promised next (Is. 9:5), with the destruction of 'every boot of the tramping warrior in battle tumult' and the burning of 'every garment rolled in blood'. 'If even the boots and cloaks are being burned, we may be sure the weapons are disposed of, and even more surely, those who wielded them' (Oswalt). The last paragraph of this prophecy indicates that this will be effected by the 'Prince of Peace' (vv. 6–7), the divine warrior of the House of David who is yet to come (cf. 11:1–9).

Application

Salvation in Old Testament prophecy is regularly portrayed in military terms because Israel's oppression was physical and political. Furthermore, God's covenant promises to bless national Israel and make her a blessing to the nations could not be fulfilled while she was under such oppression and attack.

But as we read on, we realize that the messianic deliverance needs to be at a more profound level. The real problem in Israel was spiritual and moral (e.g. Is. 8:5–22; 9:8 – 10:4). The end of war signals the end of divine punishment by armies and battles. This implies the introduction of some other way of dealing with the problem of sin. The coming Davidic king will exercise a rule of wisdom, righteousness and truth (11:1–5), bringing a transformed creation and an earth full of the knowledge of the Lord (11:6–9). Later prophecies speak in more detail of the effect of God's saving intervention on the attitude and behaviour of his people (e.g. 30:19–22; 32:1–8; 35:1–10).

From the New Testament it is clear that Jesus' death, resurrection and heavenly exaltation achieve the promised salvation. He fulfils the sin-bearing role of the Servant of the Lord in Isaiah 53, taking the punishment due for the sin of others (cf. Mark 10:45; Luke 22:37; Rom. 3:21–26). Thus he removes the 'burden' of sin and its consequences. He overcomes death and all the powers of evil, Satan is 'cast out' and people from all nations are drawn to serve the glorified Christ (e.g. John 12:31–32; Col. 2:15; Heb. 2:14–15). Thus he defeats the great 'oppressor' and delivers people from his rule. Repentance and the forgiveness of sins can be proclaimed in Christ's name to all nations, and the Holy Spirit is poured out on those who acknowledge Jesus as Lord and Christ (e.g. Luke 24:45–49; Acts 2:32–39).

Of course, wars and oppression continue in our world because Jesus' salvation is not received and his kingly rule is rejected by so many (cf. Mark 13:7–8). But where his 'yoke' is accepted (cf. Matt. 11:28–30), the transformation anticipated by the prophets begins to be experienced. And this is a clear sign that the complete deliverance from sin and all its effects will be experienced when Jesus returns in glory to restore all things (cf. Mark 13:24–27; Acts 3:19–21).

Isaiah 9:3–5 points us to the way God brings joy into our lives, as he removes the burden of sin and its consequences, delivers us from the rule of Satan, the great oppressor, and transforms our lives through Christ. This is what happens when the light of Christ shines into our darkness (cf. vv. 1–2).

3. The God who establishes the rule of his Son to fulfil his saving purposes (Is. 9:6–7)

> [6]For to us a child is born,
>   to us a son is given;
> and the government shall be upon his shoulder,
>   and his name shall be called
> Wonderful Counsellor, Mighty God,
>   Everlasting Father, Prince of Peace.
> [7]Of the increase of his government and of peace
>   there will be no end,
> on the throne of David and over his kingdom,
>   to establish it and to uphold it
> with justice and with righteousness
>   from this time forth and for evermore.
> The zeal of the LORD of hosts will do this.

Four children are mentioned in Isaiah 7 – 9, each with God-given names to reveal God's purposes. This one is clearly a royal person, though he is never actually called 'king'. In him the divine promise to David is ultimately fulfilled (2 Sam. 7:12–16):

> When your days are fulfilled and you lie down with your fathers, I will raise up your offspring after you, who shall come from your body, and I will establish his kingdom. He shall build a house for my name, and I will establish the throne of his kingdom for ever. I will be to him a father, and he shall be to me a son. When he commits iniquity, I will discipline him with the rod of men, with the stripes of the sons of men, but my steadfast love will not depart from him, as I took it from Saul, whom I put away from before you. And your house and your kingdom shall be made sure for ever before me. Your throne shall be established for ever.

The coming ruler is to be 'a son' for David and, in a sense, a son for all Israel. But, because of God's promise to David, he is also a son to God (cf. 2 Sam. 7:14). He is truly human ('to us a child is born'), though he is also divine because of the fourfold name by which he is to be called ('Wonderful Counsellor, Mighty God, Everlasting Father, Prince of Peace').

Oswalt writes that the names given to this fourth child

no longer express some future event or situation as do Shear-jashub and Maher-shalal-hash-baz. Neither do they directly express the relation between God and his people, as does Immanuel. Rather, they express the remarkable nature of this individual and thus, indirectly, the saving character of his reign. In this respect, he is the ultimate expression of the truth that God is indeed with us (Immanuel), not for our destruction, but for our redemption.

Beginning with the word 'for' (Is. 9:6), the prophet gives the ultimate reason why God's people will be able to 'rejoice' before him (v. 3). It has to do with the birth of a particular 'child', the gift of a particular 'son'. 'The emphasis falls not on what the child will do when grown up but on the mere fact of his birth. In his coming all that results from his coming is at once secured' (Motyer). The 'government' that shall be 'upon his shoulders' is an everlasting rule, involving eternal 'peace' and perfect 'justice' (v. 7).

The birth-name by which 'he shall be called' is fourfold, suggesting 'the ultimate deity of this child-deliverer' (Oswalt). Some commentators seek to avoid this conclusion, making the king a mere representative of God on earth.[2] This approach is unsatisfactory, especially with reference to the second and third titles. At the very least, these titles express key truths about the Lord

---

2. Thus, the first name is said to signify that his plans will attain their goal 'because God guides his thoughts', the second emphasizes 'the fulness of his power' as 'the legitimate representative of God upon earth', the third describes his 'enduring, fatherly, beneficent, and righteous rule', without suggesting the immortality of the king himself, and the fourth his role as the one who brings to the world 'an all-embracing and never-ending

God, who is committed to working through the son of David, so that his reign will bring peace and justice (Goldingay). But 'Prince of Peace' is surely a description of the coming king and not of the Lord who sends him. In other words, the first three titles point to the divinity of the one whose role as 'Prince of Peace' is then more fully explained in verse 7.

'Wonderful Counsellor' (lit. 'wonder of a counsellor') means either 'a supernatural counsellor' or 'one giving supernatural counsel' (Motyer). Isaiah constantly derides the foolishness of human wisdom and what it achieves (e.g. 5:21; 19:11–15; 28:7–10; 29:9–14). Such counsellors are to be replaced by one who is himself the source of divine wisdom (cf. 11:2). The Lord of hosts is described as 'wonderful in counsel' in 28:29 (cf. 25:1; 29:14).

'Mighty God' (Hebrew *'ēl gibbôr*) is a term used in the next chapter to refer to the Lord God of Israel (Is. 10:21; cf. Deut. 10:17; Jer. 32:18). The coming king will display God's own might and power in his person and life. He will be the ultimate expression of 'God with us'. As the divine 'warrior', he will accomplish the victory outlined in Isaiah 9:4–5 and bring perfect peace. The God who acted to save 'on the day of Midian' (v. 4; cf. Judg. 6 – 7) will be at work in and through this person.

'Everlasting Father' points again to the divinity of this kingly figure, emphasizing his eternity and care for his people (cf. Is. 1:2, where God's fatherly care for Israel is highlighted). The fatherhood of earthly kings was limited by death, but this king would reign 'for evermore' (Is. 9:7), perpetually expressing the fatherhood of God to his people (cf. Pss. 68:5; 103:13; Prov. 3:12; Is. 63:16; 64:8).

'Prince of Peace' could mean that he is a ruler characterized by peace but also that he brings peace. Given the broad application of the Hebrew word *šālôm* in the Old Testament, it is likely that

---

salvation' (O. Kaiser, *Isaiah 1 – 12: A Commentary* [ET, London: SCM, 1972], pp. 129–130). Motyer makes some important observations with reference to this sort of interpretation (pp. 104–105).

'Peace' here includes reconciliation with God, consequent goodwill and harmony between human beings and complete well-being in a restored creation (cf. Is. 11:6–9). His 'government' or princely rule will 'increase', and with it the 'peace' which he brings (9:7), suggesting a comparison, but ultimately a contrast with the achievement of David's son Solomon (cf. 1 Kgs. 3 – 11). 'There will be no end' to the rule of this son of David.

As Isaiah looks into the future, he perceives things happening 'from this time forth and for evermore'. Like someone examining a distant mountain through a telescope, he sees this decisive, world-transforming reign as near. When it is inaugurated, nothing will destroy its influence and nothing will replace it. Only 'the zeal of the Lord of hosts' can accomplish such a great salvation. God's 'zeal' or 'jealousy' for his people is 'the passionate commitment of his nature to fulfil his purposes for them' (Motyer; cf. Is. 37:32; 42:13; 59:17; 63:15). The love which desires their total and exclusive love for him will not rest until everything promised has been established.

Application

The last verse reminds us that the focus of this passage is on the faithfulness of God to his promises and his people. God's zealous yearning for his people will ultimately bring about their complete salvation. So he must be trusted in the present, whatever the darkness, because his light will shine and his ultimate deliverance will be experienced in a kingdom of eternal peace and justice. But the most amazing thing about this passage is the revelation of the way God will fulfil his promises in one who is uniquely 'God with us'. From now on, Israel's hope and confidence for salvation is linked explicitly with the promise of divine kingship, to be exercised by a new 'David'. The vision was recorded to give this specific hope to believers in the prophet's own generation and beyond.

Together with the parallel passage, which speaks about the Spirit of the Lord resting on this kingly figure to enable him to fulfil his ministry (Is. 11:1–5), the prophecy of Isaiah 9:6–7 reveals something of the glory of God as Trinity. The humanity and the divinity of the deliverer are affirmed together. In line with the prediction of 2 Samuel 7:14, this son of David is also the Son of God, but in a deeper sense than that foundational promise suggests. His fourfold name indicates that he manifests and expresses the supernatural wisdom, the conquering power, the everlasting fatherly care and the saving peace of the Lord God of Israel. Established by 'the Lord of hosts' himself, his reign will never end. It will be the means by which God as Father, Son and Holy Spirit fulfils his creative and redemptive purposes, for Israel and the nations.

There are many passages in the New Testament pointing to the fulfilment of Isaiah's vision in the person and work of the Lord Jesus Christ, even though the text itself is not cited. Zechariah's prophecy speaks about God visiting and redeeming his people, raising up 'a horn of salvation for us in the house of his servant David' (Luke 1:68–69). The angel of the Lord proclaims to the shepherds near Bethlehem, 'unto you is born this day in the city of David a Saviour who is Christ the Lord' (Luke 2:11). Jesus himself challenges his contemporaries to explain how the scribes can say that the Christ is the son of David when David, inspired by the Holy Spirit in Psalm 110:1, calls him Lord (Mark 12:35–37).

The apostle Peter preaches that Jesus' resurrection, ascension and pouring out of the Holy Spirit demonstrate that he is 'both Lord and Christ', the one who fulfils David's predictions in Psalms 16:8–11 and 110:1 (Acts 2:24–36). For Paul, the gospel of God is all about 'his Son, who was descended from David according to the flesh and was declared to be the Son of God in power according to the Spirit of holiness by his resurrection from the dead, Jesus Christ our Lord' (Rom. 1:3–4).

Hebrews 1 speaks about the Son of God as 'the radiance of the glory of God and the exact imprint of his nature'. As the one appointed 'the heir of all things', he inaugurates his redemptive rule through suffering and heavenly exaltation, thus fulfilling a raft of scriptures including 2 Samuel 7:14 and Psalm 110:1. In visions of the heavenly throne room, John identifies the one seated at the right hand of God as 'the Lion of the tribe of Judah, the Root of David' (Rev. 5:5). As the Lamb who was slain, he has already conquered, having 'ransomed people for God from every tribe and language and people and nation' (Rev. 5:9). But the saints on earth still await the end of persecution and pain, when God's judgments are complete, and those who endure in faith can enter into the inheritance secured for them by the triumphant Son of God (Rev. 19 – 22).

For Christians, therefore, Isaiah 9:6–7 is a mini-creed, proclaiming the character of Jesus Christ and his kingdom. Each element of the fourfold name invites us to consider something different about the one who is appointed to rule over us. As the third part of the hymn of praise to God which began in verse 4, this paragraph invites us to rejoice before him and to be glad that he rules in a world of darkness, oppression and war. God rules in the one whom we acknowledge as the Son of David and the Son of God.

6   God's People Under Judgment
(Isaiah 9:8 – 10:4)

Christianity is often dismissed as a comfort for old age or a lifeline for people in distress. It is widely regarded as being irrelevant to everyday life and unnecessary for strong, coping people. Of course, there is a profoundly comforting and consoling aspect to the gospel and to the Christian life. But that is not the whole story! God's word is full of challenge, rebuke and warning – for individuals, for churches, and for societies. God confronts us through his word spoken and his word enacted and demands a response from all his creatures. When we ignore him, we are assured that his wrath will be experienced, in the immediate consequences of our rebellion and in the final encounter with God that is the last judgment.

Isaiah 9:8 – 10:4 presents a profoundly disturbing warning to a community on the slippery slope to self-destruction. It has something to say to our wider society, but we have to remember that it is addressed in the first place to those claiming to be the people of God. We must ask what it says to us as churches, because God's great concern is for the holiness or distinctness of his people, as they seek to be his witnesses in the world.

The prophecy is in a poetic form, with four stanzas ending with the same refrain (9:12b, 17b, 21b; 10:4b). It reveals a process of decline and explains why it happens. The poem is similar in form and content to the message delivered against the southern kingdom of Judah in Isaiah 5:8–25. But it is directed to the northern kingdom (here represented by the leading tribe of Ephraim and the capital Samaria, 9:9), showing Isaiah's concern for the divided people of Israel as a whole. The prophet speaks about a process of judgment already at work but soon to have its climax on a particular 'day of punishment'. We will explore the parallel with New Testament teaching about present expressions of the wrath of God culminating in Christ's return.

1. Judgment for arrogant optimism (Is. 9:8–12)

> [8]The Lord has sent a word against Jacob,
>> and it will fall on Israel;
> [9]and all the people will know,
>> Ephraim and the inhabitants of Samaria,
>> who say in pride and in arrogance of heart:
> [10]'The bricks have fallen,
>> but we will build with dressed stones;
> the sycamores have been cut down,
>> but we will put cedars in their place.'
> [11]But the LORD raises the adversaries of
>> Rezin against him,
>> and stirs up his enemies.
> [12]The Syrians on the east and the Philistines
>> on the west
>> devour Israel with open mouth.
> For all this his anger has not turned away,
>> and his hand is stretched out still.

The key to understanding the whole passage is 9:8–9b. NRSV has translated the Hebrew entirely in the past tense (which is possible).

But ESV (with NIV, Oswalt and Webb) reads: 'The Lord has sent a word against Jacob and *it will fall* on Israel; and all the people *will know*'.

The tenses of the verbs throughout the poem are mixed. This suggests that we are not intended to distinguish between 'events which happened before, during or after the time at which the words were spoken' (Webb). In other words, God has sent his message of warning (through Isaiah and the prophets who came before him). The people are in the process of rejecting that word and experiencing the consequences of that rejection.[1] The process is far from over, since God's 'hand is stretched out still' (9:12, NIV 'still upraised')!

We should also note that 'word' (Heb. *dāḇār*) means a message or decree, but also the event or happening which God predicts and commands. The word which the Lord has sent almost seems to have 'a life of its own; *it will fall on Israel* with devastating results' (Webb). God's word would be experienced as inspired proclamation and prediction, but also as event and fulfilment. Israel would 'know' the word of the Lord in both these ways and would still deny it and reject God's call to faith and obedience.

According to 9:9–10, the fundamental reason for this denial and rejection is arrogant optimism. Ephraim and the inhabitants of Samaria would 'speak in pride and in arrogance of heart' about rebuilding everything destroyed in the judgment of God. We all admire the incredible optimism that enables people to rebuild their lives, to restore their property and to restart their businesses after terrible tragedy – floods, fire, war or disease. But when that optimism is expressed in denial of the warning that God is sending, it is arrogant and foolish – a slippery slide to further disaster and ultimate judgment.

So even when the Lord sent the Syrians on the east and the Philistines on the west to 'devour Israel with open mouth' (9:12),

---

1. 'The descriptions of the nation and its fate are spoken in the interval between the issuing of the decree in heaven and its implementation on earth' (Webb).

they still would not repent and seek after him. Their natural inclination was simply to rebuild after the tragedy and to leave God out of the picture. Pride and self-confidence were their watchword, but God could not simply ignore their response. 'For all this, his anger has not turned away, and his hand is stretched out still.'

Application

The apostle Peter warns about judgment beginning 'at the household of God' (1 Pet. 4:17) and, in so doing, suggests a continuity and progression in God's dealings with Israel and, through Christ, with the church. He refers to the suffering of persecution that was coming upon his readers because of their commitment to Christ (1 Pet. 4:12–16). This was not a punishment for their sin, though the apostle was concerned that some might suffer for any crime or inconsistency of behaviour, rather than for their Christian confession. Furthermore, he asks, if judgment begins with the church, 'what will be the outcome for those who do not obey the gospel of God?'

Peter's warning reflects the broader pattern of prophetic preaching about judgment beginning with God's people and in God's own temple (e.g. Jer. 25:29–32; Ezek. 9:5–6; Mal. 3:1–6; 4:1–6).[2] In Isaiah 10:5–12, the prophet speaks of God's judgment on the godless nation of Assyria, after he has used Assyria to express his wrath against Jerusalem and Samaria. Only a remnant of Israel will survive the purifying judgment of God. In Isaiah 9:8 – 10:4, the outpouring of divine displeasure against Israel begins. In the macro–typology of the Bible, this whole process prefigures the ultimate judgment of Jesus Christ, which begins with the church and moves on to involve the whole created order and all who live in it (e.g. Matt. 13:24–30, 36–43; 25:14–46; 2 Thess. 1:6–10; Rev. 6 – 19).

The apostle Paul speaks more generally about present expressions

---

2. P. H. Davids notes how this theme was developed as a concept of purifying judgment in Intertestamental Judaism and then in the New Testament (*The First Epistle of Peter*, NICNT [Grand Rapids: Eerdmans, 1990], p. 171).

of the wrath of God 'against all ungodliness and unrighteousness of men, who by their unrighteousness suppress the truth' (Rom. 1:18). His focus is not the church but all who 'knew God', but did not 'honour him as God or give thanks to him', but 'became futile in their thinking, and their foolish hearts were darkened' (v. 21). Later in the passage, after describing the unrighteousness that flows from suppressing the truth about God (vv. 22–31), he concludes, 'Though they know God's decree that those who practise such things deserve to die, they not only do them but give approval to those who practise them' (v. 32).

Like Isaiah, Paul sees the wrath of God being expressed in everyday present experience. Three times he says, 'God gave them up' (vv. 24, 26, 28), meaning literally that God 'handed over' humanity to the consequences of its rejection of him. But neither Isaiah nor Paul is simply talking about 'a natural process of cause and effect',[3] which God has built into the universe. God's wrath is a personal expression of his anger against sin (e.g. Exod. 32:7–10; Josh. 23:15–16; Pss. 59:12–13; 69:24; Is. 10:24–25). It does not occur in fitful outbursts, such as we might display towards those who upset us. It is a measured and predictable response by the Creator to the rebellion of his creatures. Present manifestations of God's wrath are a warning of greater things to come (cf. Rom. 2:3–5).

Of course, every negative experience that people have is not to be measured as a particular expression of God's wrath to the individuals concerned. The book of Job warns us about making such simplistic conclusions. In our fallen world, the innocent sometimes suffer and the ungodly sometimes escape any serious punishment. However, God's wrath against human sin collectively is revealed in the sort of events portrayed by Isaiah, and individuals get caught up in the consequences. How foolish it is to know

---

3. C. H. Dodd argued this way and sought to avoid the conclusion that wrath is expressed in a direct act of God against sinners (*The Epistle of Paul to the Romans* [London: Fontana, 1959], pp. 50–55).

something of God and his will – even to experience his judgment against sin in some practical and personal way – and not to turn to him in repentance and faith.

In the light of New Testament teaching about the judgment of Christ, how might we apply Isaiah 9:8–12 to the church? The prophet's assumption is that the people of God ought to be those who believe the warnings of God and discern the signs of his wrath in the affairs of life. But pride and arrogance of heart produce a stubborn resistance to the will of God and blind people to the significance of what is going on about them. In the contemporary scene, we see declining numbers in many churches, moral outrage at the behaviour of some clergy, financial crises in the denominations and diminishing influence on the life of the nation. But these facts seem to make little impact on those who think they can rebuild the church in their own strength and survive by their own wisdom.

We need to be humbled and brought to repentance by every sign of the wrath of God against the church of our day. Only in this way can we become urgent, insistent and convincing proclaimers of God's judgment to the world. If we fail to proclaim the gospel of God's final judgment to our neighbours then, humanly speaking, they will have little hope of being saved through faith in Christ.

2. Judgment for misguided leadership (Is. 9:13–17)

[13]The people did not turn to him who struck them,
> nor enquire of the LORD of hosts.
[14]So the LORD cut off from Israel head and tail,
> palm branch and reed in one day –
[15]the elder and honoured man is the head,
> and the prophet who teaches lies is the tail;
[16]for those who guide this people have been leading them astray,
> and those who are guided by them are swallowed up.
[17]Therefore the Lord does not rejoice over their young men,
> and has no compassion on their fatherless and widows;
> for everyone is godless and an evildoer,

> and every mouth speaks folly.
> For all this his anger has not turned away,
>> and his hand is stretched out still.

If the first stanza of this prophetic poem is about the people in general, the second is fundamentally about those who led them (v. 16). The pride and arrogance of heart manifested in verse 10 prevented the people from turning 'to him who struck them' and enquiring of the Lord of hosts (v. 13). God declares his intention to 'cut off from Israel head and tail, palm branch and reed in one day' (v. 14) – an event presumably still to come (NIV translates 'will cut off').

This last verse is clearly a reference to the totality of the leadership in the land. 'Head and tail' are explained in the next verse: 'the elder and honored man is the head, and the prophet who teaches lies is the tail' (v. 15). Political and religious leaders are included together in this accusation. Church and state are intricately linked in God's dealings with Israel. False prophets are 'the tail' that is wagging the dog here, by teaching lies (v. 15).[4] In a theocracy, they have the greatest responsibility and the greatest opportunity for influencing the life of the community, by challenging the political leaders with God's revealed word.

The result of such false teaching and such misguided leadership is that the people as a whole are led astray. Indeed, 'those who are guided by them are swallowed up' (v. 16). This is seen in different areas of society – 'their young men, their fatherless and widows' all suffer (v. 17). At one level, the problem is described in terms of human failure: 'everyone is godless and an evildoer, and every mouth speaks folly'. At another level, this is God's judgment on his people: 'the Lord does not rejoice over their young men, and has

---

4. Alternatively, the meaning is that they were 'like tails wagging at public demand (cf. 30:9–11; 1 Ki. 22:6; Mi. 2:11)' (Motyer). Rather than influencing the political leaders with strong, clear direction, they were simply prophesying to please.

no compassion on their fatherless and widows' (v. 17).

So the problem here is God's failure to intervene and rescue the ordinary members of society from the effects of such false teaching and misguided leadership. Evil abounds and God appears to be silent! But this is as much a demonstration of his wrath as the sudden and complete removal of these leaders, 'in one day' (v. 14). The Lord is about to remove them in a way that demonstrates his wrath even more obviously. 'For all this, his anger has not turned away, and his hand is stretched out still.'

Application

Such passages directed to the community of God's people under the Mosaic Covenant speak first to the church under the New Covenant. If Isaiah 9:8–12 points to the judgment God brings upon the church for its pride and arrogance, 9:13–17 warns of the particular judgment he brings on the leaders of his people who fail to teach and live the truth. In simple terms, they will be 'cut off'. This may happen as scandals are exposed and leaders are deposed. It may happen as leaders lose respect and influence because of their unfaithfulness. Moreover, there may be a famine of 'hearing the words of the Lord' (Amos 8:11), as professing Christians become disinterested in or actually hostile to the word of God because of the neglect of pastors to teach it with conviction and clarity.

We do not live in a theocracy, but the influence of Christian teachers and preachers on the political and social life of a nation can still be profound. When we look at the corruption and suffering in our society, we must accept some responsibility for it. Christian witness is often muted because many want to modify the gospel to suit the culture, rather than challenging the culture with the unadulterated word of God. Positively, we need to encourage Christian leaders to have a prophetic-type ministry, with reference to moral and social issues. Whether they hear or refuse to hear, the community at large ought to be faced with God's standards and with their own accountability before God.

In the final analysis, Isaiah 9 shows the need for the kind of leadership in our churches that will enable God's people to live in holiness and to serve him faithfully (cf. 1 Pet. 5:1–5). Such leadership will be morally responsible, caring for every individual in the church, concerned to reflect God's standards and values in personal discipleship and in the life of the congregation.

3. Judgment for mutual exploitation (Is. 9:18–21)

¹⁸For wickedness burns like a fire;
> it consumes briers and thorns;
> it kindles the thickets of the forest,
> and they roll upwards in a column of smoke.
¹⁹Through the wrath of the LORD of hosts
> the land is scorched,
> and the people are like fuel for the fire;
> no one spares another.
²⁰They slice meat on the right, but are still hungry,
> and they devour on the left, but are not satisfied;
> each devours the flesh of his own arm,
²¹Manasseh devours Ephraim,
> and Ephraim devours Manasseh;
> together they are against Judah.
> For all this his anger has not turned away,
> and his hand is stretched out still.

The multiplication of evil is likened to 'a fire' which 'consumes briers and thorns' (v. 18). This is a powerful image, considering the destructive effect of brush or forest fires. It is a way of saying that the spread of evil is an expression of 'the wrath of the LORD of hosts' (v. 19). He does not intervene to stop it. When the prophet talks about 'the land' being scorched, he means that 'the people' are destroyed. They become 'like fuel for the fire'.

So false teaching and misguided leadership lead to moral decay, and the outcome of that is social disintegration. There is a process of decline to be observed here. When the knowledge of God is rejected, there is nothing to control or direct human relationships in the way that God would have them function. Proclaiming that 'the people are like fuel for the fire', the prophet goes straight on to say, 'no one spares another' (v. 19b). This is explained with the graphic image of people devouring one another and never being satisfied by it (vv. 20–21). They are so insatiable and greedy that they actually end up devouring themselves ('each devours the flesh of his own arm')![5]

As well as exploiting one another in everyday-life situations, the prophet speaks of war between spiritual brothers ('Manasseh devours Ephraim, and Ephraim devours Manasseh; together they are against Judah'), a reference again to hostility between the tribes of Israel. And, for all this destruction of relationships and social disharmony, 'his anger has not turned away, and his hand is stretched out still'. God has not finished judging such wayward people.

Application

Once again, the prophet makes us consider the social consequences of rebellion against God. He challenges us to look first at the church, then at the world in which we live. He shows how the rejection of a right relationship with God leads to a spoiling of human relationships at every level. Mutual exploitation and hostility among professing Christians are signs that they are out of touch with God and his will (cf. 1 John 3:11–17). A passage such as James 4:1–12 indicates that quarrels and fights among believers or slander expressed against one another are signs of enmity with God, friendship with the world and submission to the devil!

In society at large, it is not simply a lack of education or health care, natural resources or wealth that causes human misery. There are deeper, theological reasons for the problems of our world. Once again Isaiah reminds us of the way in which God expresses his

---

5. The ESV translation is more literal than the NIV here ('each will feed on the flesh of his own offspring').

wrath in abandoning people to the consequences of their rebellion against him. The apostle Paul similarly reminds us that the strife and deceit that spoil human relationships are rooted in our refusal to acknowledge God as God (Rom. 1:28–32). God allows people to go their own way (vv. 24, 26, 28), 'in order that they might at last learn from their consequent wretchedness to hate the futility of a life turned away from the truth of God'.[6] The cruelty, injustice and destruction we practise on one another are signs that humanity is out of touch with God and his purpose in creating us. Life was not meant to be this way!

Furthermore, Romans 2:4 makes it clear that God's withholding of the ultimate judgment for our sin is an expression of his kindness, which is meant to lead us to repentance. But those who remain hard and impenitent in the face of God's present judgments are 'storing up wrath for themselves on the day of wrath when God's righteous judgement will be revealed' (v. 5).

4. Judgment for corrupt law-makers (Is. 10:1–4)

[1]Woe to those who decree iniquitous decrees,
    and the writers who keep writing oppression,
[2]to turn aside the needy from justice
    and to rob the poor of my people of their right,
 that widows may be their spoil,
    and that they may make the fatherless their prey!
[3]What will you do on the day of punishment,
    in the ruin that will come from afar?
 To whom will you flee for help,
    and where will you leave your wealth?
[4]Nothing remains but to crouch among the prisoners
    or fall among the slain.

---

6. C. E. B. Cranfield, *A Critical and Exegetical Commentary on the Epistle to the Romans*, Vol. 1 (ICC, Edinburgh: T. & T. Clark, 1975), p. 121.

> For all this his anger has not turned away,
> and his hand is stretched out still.

Two things are probably involved in 10:1–2. The enactment of unjust laws ('Woe to those who decree iniquitous decrees') is coupled with the idea of applying laws in a grievous or oppressive way ('the writers who keep writing oppression').[7] In contemporary terms we may say that politicians and judges are on view together. The things listed in verse 2 were explicitly prohibited by the law of Moses: turning aside 'the needy from justice' and robbing 'the poor of my people of their right'. Acting to put right such situations was meant to be a reflection of the character and care of God himself (cf. Exod. 23:6–9; Lev. 19:15; Deut. 10:17; 16:19; 24:17). This was to be a special responsibility of the leaders of Israel.

The injustice that was being practised, however, was designed to make widows 'their spoil' and the fatherless 'their prey'! Depriving the helpless of their rights in order to oppress them is completely self-serving and the ultimate expression of arrogance against God. Here is a specific example of what Isaiah means by people devouring one another (Is. 9:20). When we see such exploitation of the weak by the strong we realize how awful sin is. Such behaviour is no different from the bullying that many children experience in the school playground! The prophet has already shown us that the deep-rooted cause of this is the rejection of God and his word by individuals and society.

That is why 'the day of punishment', which is yet to come, is such a serious prospect for such people (Is. 10:3–4). Those who have been in positions of power will have no-one to flee to for help ('To whom will you flee for help?'). There will be no way of protecting the wealth they have acquired illegitimately ('where will you leave your wealth?'). There will be no special favours, but only the

---

7. NIV, 'Woe to those who make unjust laws, to those who issue oppressive decrees.'

prospect of being punished with everyone else ('to crouch among the prisoners or fall among the slain'). Even so, 'for all this, his anger has not turned away, and his hand is stretched out still'. Isaiah leaves us with the impression that even the Assyrian invasion will not be sufficient to satisfy God's wrath against such rebellious people. There is something worse to come. The God of justice takes such injustice seriously and he will repay (cf. Prov. 20:22; Rom. 12:19).

Application

It is significant that Isaiah has two messages of warning for community leaders (Is. 9:13–17; 10:1–4), following two messages for the people in general (9:8–12, 18–21). This shows unmistakably the responsibility of such leaders for the spiritual condition and general plight of the people, without excusing in any way the people for their own part in this sorry situation. Since we have argued that a passage like this must be applied to the church first, we must ask how the sort of injustice and oppression observed by the prophet is evidenced in the leadership of our churches.

It is certainly possible for church leaders to use their position to accumulate riches and to seek power for themselves. This will inevitably be at the expense of those they are called to serve. Church laws and the way in which they are administered can 'turn aside the needy from justice' and rob the poor of their right in a whole range of practical situations. Instead of modelling biblical ideals, churches can be no better than secular institutions in their lack of care for the welfare of those who are most vulnerable and in need. Isaiah challenges us to expose such corruption and to call such leaders to repent.

As we conclude this examination of Isaiah 9:8 – 10:4, with its portrait of God's people under judgment, it is important to notice the context in which the prophet presents his denunciation and warning. It comes immediately after the amazing disclosure of the coming of the promised Son of David, to bring light and joy, deliverance from oppression and judgment, perfect peace and an eternal rule of wisdom and righteousness (9:1–7; cf. 11:1–16). It is soon followed by another promise about the salvation of a remnant of the Israelites (10:20–27). In other words, Isaiah's preaching about judgment is in the context of his teaching about God's grace. This again is Paul's pattern in Romans 1 – 3. It is an important warning to us about the way to proclaim the awesome truths of God's justice and wrath, with a focus on Christ as Redeemer and merciful Saviour.

7 God's Strange Work
(Isaiah 10:5–34)

The idea that God should punish people for their sins seems strange to many. They imagine him as a heavenly grandfather, who dotes over us and simply says 'There, there' when we do wrong! Such a view falls short of the revelation God has given to us of his holiness and righteousness. But even more strange is the perspective of Isaiah 10:5–34. Here the prophet envisages Assyria being the instrument of God for punishing Israel in the eighth century BC. But Assyria knows nothing of this and in due course must be punished for her own sin. Even more mysteriously, God will use the judgment falling on most of his people at this time as the means by which he saves a few.

How can this be fair and just? Does God use people as puppets, only to throw them away when they have fulfilled his purpose? How can the punishment of one group lead to the salvation of another? Does this prophecy have any parallel or fulfilment in the New Testament? Isaiah makes us think carefully about the interplay between God's sovereignty and human responsibility, but also about the way his justice and his mercy operate together.

There are three broad divisions in this passage, where the focus is on Assyria first (10:5–19), then on 'the remnant' in Israel (10:20–27), and finally on Assyria again (10:28–34). Webb notes that each of these divisions has two subsections: A (5–11, 12–19), B (20–23, 24–27) and A' (28–32, 33–34), each of which has a different emphasis. The link between the first main division and the preceding prophecy is the word 'anger' in verses 4 and 5. A similar link between the first and second divisions of this passage is provided by the word 'remnant' in verses 19 and 20. Such links show how these sections of Isaiah's work belong together and identify the main theme of those sections.

1. Punishing the instruments of his judgment (Is. 10:5–19)

a. Conflicting agendas: Assyria and God

> ⁵Ah, Assyria, the rod of my anger;
>> the staff in their hands is my fury!
> ⁶Against a godless nation I send him,
>> and against the people of my wrath I command him,
> to take spoil and seize plunder,
>> and to tread them down like the mire of the streets.
> ⁷But he does not so intend,
>> and his heart does not so think;
> but it is in his heart to destroy,
>> and to cut off nations not a few;
> ⁸for he says:
>> 'Are not my commanders all kings?
> ⁹Is not Calno like Carchemish?
>> Is not Hamath like Arpad?
>> Is not Samaria like Damascus?
> ¹⁰As my hand has reached to the kingdoms of the idols,
>> whose carved images were greater than those
>> of Jerusalem and Samaria,
> ¹¹shall I not do to Jerusalem and her idols
>> as I have done to Samaria and her images?'

Assyria is startlingly addressed as 'the rod of my anger' (v. 5). From God's perspective, 'the staff in their hands is my fury!'[1] So when the Assyrians go forth to pursue their own policy of military and political aggression, God will actually use them as an instrument of judgment against his chosen people. This will happen because Israel is 'a godless nation' and 'the people of my wrath' (v. 6), fully deserving of the judgment that is coming upon them. Such a description of Israel is ironic because the Israelites doubtless thought of the Assyrians as the most godless and profane people on the face of the earth. In God's eyes, however, Israel was no different, having abandoned the relationship with God that he had made possible.[2]

God does not simply 'allow' Assyria to fulfil his purpose – as if this is a convenient outworking of historical circumstances for God! Speaking as the mouthpiece of the Lord, Isaiah says, 'I send him' and 'I command him' (v. 6). Although he does not speak openly to him and reveal his purposes to him, the Lord initiates and directs what the king of Assyria thinks he is doing in his own wisdom and strength.[3]

It is God's specific will for Assyria 'to take spoil and seize plunder, and to tread them down like the mire of the streets'. So at this point God's will and Assyria's intentions appear to coincide. God's anger against Israel will soon be expressed in certain precise historic events. But the prophet goes on to say that Assyria 'does not so

---

1. Motyer observes that this last expression could mean that 'the Lord's anger empowers Assyria'.
2. Oswalt comments that Jesus' words, 'Everyone to whom much was given, of him much will be required, and from him to whom they entrusted much, they will demand the more' (Luke 12:48), apply to Israel and Assyria. 'Relatively speaking, Israel is more profane and godless than Assyria because she has had more light to reject.'
3. Compare the prophecy directed to Cyrus king of Persia (Is. 45:1–13), which speaks about this ruler as one who does not know the Lord, but who will nevertheless be the instrument of God's salvation for the remnant of Israel.

intend, and his heart does not so think' (v. 7). Her godless leader is set
on annihilation ('it is in his heart to destroy') and world domination
('to cut off nations not a few'). Assyria is portrayed as saying
that *Samaria*, representing the northern kingdom, and *Jerusalem*,
representing the southern kingdom, will be a push-over compared
with previous victories (vv. 8–11).

The arrogant boasting of the king of Assyria begins with the
claim that 'kings' of captured nations have all become 'commanders'
who do his will (v. 8). Six cities are then mentioned in pairs, suggesting
an inexorable movement of the conquering empire southwards to
Samaria (v. 9).[4] Next, Jerusalem is singled out for attack (vv. 10–11),
thus fulfilling the pattern of overflowing judgment predicted in
8:5–8. These two cities and the kingdoms they represent are said to
have 'idols', but their idolatry is nothing compared to 'the kingdoms
of the idols' already defeated. In other words, Samaria and
Jerusalem are dismissed as being spiritually weak compared to the
proficient idolaters encountered elsewhere! Put another way, the
king of Assyria did not consider the God of Israel to be any more
powerful than the gods of the nations already conquered.

Application

'There is only one Agent and he does all things well. Under him,
history is the outworking of moral providences. The Assyrian
holocaust was not "let loose" on the world; it was sent, directed
where it was merited (6), kept within heaven's limits, and in the end
Assyria was punished for its excesses (12)' (Motyer). Isaiah presents a
clear picture of the absolute sovereignty of God over human history
and over the lives of individuals who do not acknowledge him. This
is not a form of divine manipulation, where human beings are
employed like puppets. The real will and intentions of Assyria are
acknowledged. But Assyria is not free to pursue its mad purpose

---

4. These conquests are listed in geographical, rather than chronological
   order, moving ever closer to Samaria and then Jerusalem.

without restraint. God can 'order the unruly wills and affections of sinful men'.[5] This is a 'longitudinal theme' in Scripture.

In Isaiah 37:28–29, this great world power is likened to a horse, with its own intentions and desires, which God must control and turn back on its way. The prophet envisions 'a God who is not the prisoner of history, who is not the alter ego of either victor or vanquished, but who guides all events to an outcome in keeping with his own joyous and beneficent plan. All are under his hand' (Oswalt).

Here we see an important illustration of the way God's sovereignty and human responsibility work together. An earlier example in Scripture is the story of Joseph being sold into slavery by his brothers because of their jealousy. But God enabled him to rise to power in Egypt, to bring about the deliverance of the sons of Israel in time of famine (Gen. 37 – 50). At the end of the story, Joseph confesses, 'As for you, you meant evil against me, but God meant it for good, to bring it about that many people should be kept alive, as they are today' (Gen. 50:20).

The climax of this interplay of divine and human wills in salvation history is the suffering and death of the Lord Jesus Christ. So Peter says to the Jews in Jerusalem on the Day of Pentecost, 'this Jesus, delivered up according to the definite plan and foreknowledge of God, you crucified and killed by the hands of lawless men' (Acts 2:23). And the Jerusalem Christians later acknowledge to God in prayer:

> Truly in this city there were gathered together against your holy servant Jesus, whom you anointed, both Herod and Pontius Pilate, along with the Gentiles and the peoples of Israel, to do whatever your hand and your plan had predestined to take place (Acts 4:27–28).

There is great comfort in the general teaching of Scripture about the way God achieves his purposes through human instruments,

---

5. Collect for the Fourth Sunday after Easter in *The Book of Common Prayer* of the Church of England (1662). Cf. Prov. 21:1.

even when they do not acknowledge him and have their own ungodly agendas. But there is special comfort in knowing that this is the way he achieved our salvation. The Son of God had to learn to trust his Father in the face of human rejection, injustice and ultimately the sentence of death (e.g. Mark 14:32–42; Heb. 5:7–10; 1 Pet. 2:22–25). His learning to trust and obey in this context was an essential part of the process by which he fulfilled the Father's will and saved us. Moreover, God's ultimate triumph over evil is guaranteed by the victory of the cross and Jesus' resurrection.

b. God's response to human arrogance

¹²When the Lord has finished all his work on Mount Zion and on Jerusalem, he will punish the speech of the arrogant heart of the king of Assyria and the boastful look in his eyes. ¹³For he says:

> 'By the strength of my hand I have done it,
> and by my wisdom, for I have understanding;
> I remove the boundaries of peoples,
> and plunder their treasures;
> like a bull I bring down those who sit on thrones.
> ¹⁴My hand has found like a nest
> the wealth of the peoples;
> and as one gathers eggs that have been forsaken,
> so I have gathered all the earth;
> and there was none that moved a wing
> or opened the mouth or chirped.'

> ¹⁵Shall the axe boast over him who hews with it,
> or the saw magnify itself against him who wields it?
> As if a rod should wield him who lifts it,
> or as if a staff should lift him who is not wood!
> ¹⁶Therefore the Lord GOD of hosts
> will send wasting sickness among his stout warriors,
> and under his glory a burning will be kindled,

like the burning of fire.
¹⁷The light of Israel will become a fire,
and his Holy One a flame,
and it will burn and devour
his thorns and briers in one day.
¹⁸The glory of his forest and of his fruitful land
the LORD will destroy, both soul and body,
and it will be as when a sick man wastes away.
¹⁹The remnant of the trees of his forest will be so few
that a child can write them down.

This section begins with a prose verse, which sums up the message of 10:5–19. There is a particular focus on 'Mount Zion' and on 'Jerusalem', arising from the reference to 'Jerusalem and Samaria' in verses 10–11. Both Assyria and God are concerned about the southern, as well as the northern kingdom of Israel. But Assyria cannot escape judgment, even though she is used by God to punish Israel. A time will come when 'the Lord has finished all his work on Mount Zion and on Jerusalem'.[6] 'The Lord' himself will determine that time because it is 'his work'. He sets bounds on the expression of his anger, even though Assyria has no intention of stopping the attack. Then will come the time to 'punish the speech of the arrogant heart of the king of Assyria and the boastful look in his eyes'.[7] Motyer rightly comments: 'What the king of Assyria did

---

6. The reference is limited by the context to the Assyrian attack portrayed in Isaiah 36 – 37 and does not include the later attack by the Babylonians.

7. NRSV is similar to ESV in rendering 'he will punish the arrogant boasting of the king of Assyria and his haughty pride'. The Hebrew is actually in the first person singular, which is why the NIV inserts the words 'he will say' and translates 'I will punish the king of Assyria for the wilful pride of his heart and the haughty look in his eyes'. It is a characteristic of the Hebrew prophets to move from speaking *about* God in the third person to speaking *for* God in the first person.

conformed to the will of God; why he did it had nothing to do with the will of God, only with the king's arrogance and vaingloriousness.'

Isaiah has much to say about human pride being humbled by God (cf. 2:9–22; 13:11; 14:13–15; 47:7–11). Assyria was not merely ignorant of the true God but blinded with arrogance and full of boasting. In the words of the king himself, every victory has been 'by the strength of my hand' and 'by my wisdom, for I have understanding' (10:13). There is no recognition of any need for God in the leader who thinks, 'I remove the boundaries of peoples, and plunder their treasures; like a bull I bring down those who sit on thrones.' People with such self-confidence attribute even the achievements of their commanders and their armies to themselves! So this ruler claims, 'My hand has found like a nest the wealth of the peoples; and as one gathers eggs that have been forsaken, so I have gathered all the earth' (v. 14). World domination has been as easy as bird-nesting, and there was no-one to stop him ('there was none that moved a wing or opened the mouth or chirped'). 'To take such a position is, in fact, to usurp the place of God' (Oswalt).

Such arrogant boasting and God-denying nonsense cannot go unchallenged. So the Lord asks, 'Shall the axe boast over him who hews with it, or the saw magnify itself against him who wields it?' (v. 15). It is laughable to think of an axe or a saw claiming to be responsible for a tree being felled or a log being shaped, as if the person using the instrument had no part to play in the process. It is even more ludicrous to imagine that 'a rod should wield him who lifts it' or 'a staff should lift him who is not wood!' These illustrations point to the difference between the instruments and those who use them. They challenge every human claim that we are independent from our Maker and that in some sense we benefit or support him, rather than the other way around (cf. Ps. 50:7–15).

God's response is first to declare the practical consequences for Assyria ('therefore the Lord God of hosts will send wasting sickness among his stout warriors', Is. 10:16). But the theological significance of this action is then revealed. 'Under his glory' probably refers to the glory of Assyria (NIV 'under his pomp'). The following verse makes it clear that it is because of God's glory that 'a burning will be kindled, like the burning of fire'. Isaiah's experience of the glory of the Lord was clearly very influential in the way he looked at the world and human affairs (6:1–5). 'For one who has seen the Lord high and lifted up, Assyria's vast army and suffocating glory meant little' (Oswalt). So the prophet envisages that 'the light of Israel will become a fire, and his Holy One a flame' (10:17). The God of Israel is acknowledged as 'the light of Israel' and as 'his Holy One'. The one whose 'light' can be revelation and life (cf. 9:1; 30:26; 60:1–17) can also be 'fire' and 'flame' to those who deny him. So God in his holiness must act against Assyria, to 'burn and devour his thorns and briers in one day'.

The imagery of destruction continues in 10:18–19. Assyria's 'glory' is 'his forest' and 'his fruitful land'. These appear to be metaphors for his warriors, since the prophet goes on to say, 'the Lord will destroy both soul and body'. Isaiah's language suggests the end of Assyria's power and life in very personal terms ('it will be as when a sick man wastes away').[8] Whether 'the remnant of the trees of his forest' refers to the devastation of his land or the decimation of his army, they will be 'so few that a child can write them down'. Divine justice will be swift, fair and unavoidable. Such must be the response of the Holy One to all human arrogance and boasting.

Application

C. S. Lewis rightly described pride as 'the great sin' which leads to every other vice: 'it is the complete anti-God state of mind'.[9] In

---

8. Motyer notes the pattern sickness-fire-fire-sickness in 10:16–18, suggesting that these are different metaphors for the same thing, namely the destruction of Assyria as a nation in every respect (so also Oswalt). '*Disease* and *fire* are the inner and outer agents of destruction and therefore represent every destroying force' (Motyer). This prediction was fulfilled between 629 and 605 BC.

9. *Mere Christianity* (London: Fontana, 1955), p. 106.

our pride, we seek to be independent of God, trying to play God ourselves. The king of Assyria is an exaggerated example of this common human condition, which is the outworking of Adam's rebellion against God in Genesis 3. Once again, we are in touch with a longitudinal theme in Scripture, and Isaiah's response to such arrogant self-confidence has a wider application. The Lord God of hosts cannot endure any denial of his right to rule over us. The Holy One of Israel cannot remain indifferent to those who refuse to glorify him. 'The haughty looks of man shall be brought low, and the lofty pride of men shall be humbled, and the Lord alone will be exalted in that day' (Is. 2:11).

From a New Testament perspective, however, 'that day' is the day of Christ, the day of final judgment. God's judgment against Assyria prefigures his ultimate response to those who rebel against him, whether they do that actively or passively. Here we must follow the way of typology in applying the passage. In Revelation 19:19 we read of 'the beast and the kings of the earth with their armies gathered to make war against him who was sitting on the horse and against his army'. This last desperate attempt to resist Christ's rule is quickly thwarted (Rev. 19:20–21; cf. 'the man of lawlessness' in 2 Thess. 2:1–11), so that he can reign supreme and be worshipped and adored for ever by those who fear him (Rev. 21 – 22).

2. Purifying a people for himself (Is. 10:20–27)

a. God's promise

[20]In that day the remnant of Israel and the survivors of the house of Jacob will no more lean on him who struck them, but will lean on the LORD, the Holy One of Israel, in truth. [21]A remnant will return, the remnant of Jacob, to the mighty God. [22]For though your people Israel be as the sand of the sea, only a remnant of them will return. Destruction is decreed, overflowing with righteousness. [23]For the Lord GOD of hosts will make a full end, as decreed, in the midst of all the earth.

The link between this passage and the preceding one is the word 'remnant'. When Assyria is reduced to a remnant (v. 19), 'in that day the remnant of Israel and the survivors of the house of Jacob will no more lean on him who struck them, but will lean on the LORD, the Holy One of Israel, in truth' (v. 20). 'In that day' is a phrase used by the prophet to identify a moment when 'God's hand is particularly seen in human history' (Oswalt; cf. 3:18; 4:1–2; 7:18, 20, 21, 23; 10:27).

There are several wonderful things to note about this promise. First, the reassurance that a remnant will be saved by God's grace (cf. 6:13). Second, the assurance that it will involve 'the survivors of the house of Jacob'. This reference to Jacob, who was the common ancestor of the twelve tribes, suggests that the remnant will be drawn from every tribe and will express God's faithfulness to fulfil his promises to Israel as a whole. Third, the text indicates a profound transformation of the remnant: they will 'no more lean on him who struck them, but will lean on the LORD, the Holy One of Israel, in truth'.

Leaning on Assyria meant being 'struck' by that mighty power – a disastrous outcome for such political and spiritual commitment. Leaning on 'the LORD, the Holy One of Israel' will involve salvation, righteousness and peace (cf. 11:1–9). To lean on the Lord 'in truth' means to lean on him consistently: an enduring trust in God is implied. Given the stubbornness of the human heart and Israel's failure to do this in the past, the implication is that God will bring about such a spiritual renewal by his own power and initiative.

The message is repeated in 10:21, in terms recalling past promises. 'A remnant will return' ('Shear-jashub') was the name which Isaiah gave to his son (7:3). Although the 'remnant' idea proclaims God's judgment, it also speaks of salvation.[10] Since the predicted 'return'

---

10. Although the term 'remnant' does not appear again until 17:3, 'it is still perhaps the most apt summary of the entire book, since it captures the interwoven themes of redemption and judgment that prevail from beginning to end' (Oswalt).

is 'to the mighty God', repentance or conversion is indicated. So the remnant will be characterized by enduring faith (10:20) and a genuine turning to the Lord (10:21; cf. 1:27). With the expression 'remnant of Jacob' Isaiah restates the promise of 10:20 that this remnant will represent the totality of Israel – the germ of a renewed people of God. 'To the mighty God' recalls the designation of the coming king from David's line in 9:6 (Hebrew *'ēl gibbôr*). Putting the two texts so closely together, Isaiah possibly meant us to understand that the remnant would be identified by their turning 'to the mighty God' in the person of the Messiah.

The promise that 'a remnant of them will return' is repeated once more in 10:22, with the qualification, 'though your people Israel be as the sand of the sea'.[11] These last words recall God's promise to multiply the sons of Israel and make them a great nation (Gen. 22:17; 32:12). But Isaiah uses the expression to remind them of the devastation that must now take place. This is because 'destruction is decreed, overflowing with righteousness'. In other words, promises of the salvation and transformation of a remnant must not lull them into a false sense of security. God's righteous judgment must take place first, until very few of them are left. Indeed, 'the Lord God of hosts will make a full end, as decreed, in the midst of all the earth'. 'The Lord will consummate what he has decreed, whether promise or threat' (Motyer).

Application

The apostle Paul quotes Isaiah 10:22–23 in Romans 9:27–28, as part of an extended explanation of God's strange work in his time. Many Israelites have not acknowledged Jesus as Lord and Christ. Paul is careful to point out the personal responsibility of all who failed to receive the offer of salvation in Jesus (9:30 – 10:21). Yet,

---

11. Against Motyer, the concessive reading of the Hebrew *kî 'im* ('though', 'even if') seems appropriate to the context, where a remnant is preserved during a devastating reduction of the nation's size and power (cf. 6:13).

through this process of unbelief, he insists that God is sovereign: 'he has mercy on whomever he wills, and he hardens whomever he wills' (9:18). Isaiah's message about only a remnant being saved is ultimately fulfilled in the gospel era. Although there was a primary fulfilment in the survival of a remnant out of the Assyrian crisis, the complete restoration and renewal of Israel predicted by the prophet did not really begin until the 'day' of Christ dawned.

Understanding that 'day' of Christ to involve the whole period from the time of his earthly ministry until his return in glory, Paul can affirm that 'there is a remnant, chosen by grace' (11:5). But the rest of Israel has been hardened (11:7), and this is an expression of God's severity in judgment (11:8–10, 22). Even so, the story does not end here! God's intention through Israel's 'trespass' is to bring salvation to the Gentiles, 'so as to make Israel jealous' (11:11). This perspective is not revealed in Isaiah 10, though we shall see that Isaiah 11 promises the Gentiles a share in the messianic salvation.

The apostle then unveils the final details of God's great plan. 'A partial hardening has come upon Israel, until the fullness of the Gentiles has come in, and then all Israel will be saved' (11:25–26). God has determined to save a full number of Gentiles (which does not mean every Gentile without exception), and only when that number has been reached will Israel's hardening be removed and the full number of Israelites be saved. This does not mean every Israelite without exception, since Paul is still thinking in terms of grace and election. But he is doubtless moved by the breadth of Isaiah's vision that the remnant will comprise 'the survivors of the house of Jacob'. Paul's point seems to be that, 'the present situation in salvation history, in which so few Jews are being saved, cannot finally do justice to the scriptural expectations about Israel's future. Something "more" is to be expected; and the "more", Paul implies, is a large-scale conversion of Jewish people at the end of this age.'[12]

---

12. D. Moo, *The Epistle to the Romans* (Grand Rapids, MI, and Cambridge: Eerdmans, 1996), p. 724. Paul is pushed beyond the vision of Is. 10:22–23

With the apostle, we can celebrate the extraordinary mercy of God in providing a way of salvation for Jews and Gentiles alike, through the death and resurrection of the Lord Jesus. With Paul, we can trust that God is continuing to work out his merciful purpose for Israel and the nations through the preaching of the gospel, until the full number of his elect children has come to Christ.

b. God's challenge

[24]'Therefore thus says the Lord GOD of hosts: 'O my people, who dwell in Zion, be not afraid of the Assyrians when they strike with the rod and lift up their staff against you as the Egyptians did. [25]For in a very little while my fury will come to an end, and my anger will be directed to their destruction. [26]And the LORD of hosts will wield against them a whip, as when he struck Midian at the rock of Oreb. And his staff will be over the sea, and he will lift it as he did in Egypt. [27]And in that day his burden will depart from your shoulder, and his yoke from your neck; and the yoke will be broken because of the fat.'

The prophet moves from promise to challenge with the word 'therefore'.[13] The promise that a 'remnant of Jacob' will pass safely through the coming judgment and 'return to the mighty God' gives some hope. 'The Lord God of hosts' will persist with Israel and fulfil his covenant purposes through the remnant. A challenge is therefore made to those whom the Lord still calls 'my people who dwell in Zion'. The challenge ('be not afraid of the Assyrians when they

---

by the wonderful promise of Is. 59:20–21, which he quotes in Rom. 11:20–21, and by the expectation of other prophetic passages about God's ultimate intentions for Israel.

13. While it is true that vv. 24–27 do not follow vv. 20–23 very closely, they link the promise that a remnant will be saved with the preceding promises about God's judgment on Assyria (vv. 12–19). In other words, they help to tie together the two strands of Isaiah's message in the passage as a whole.

strike with the rod and lift up their staff against you as the Egyptians did', 10:24) recalls the oppression of the Israelites by the Egyptians in the time of Moses (Exod. 1 – 6). If God delivered his people from such fearsome opponents in the past, he can do so again.

Once again, they are reminded that faith in God means not being 'afraid' of their enemies (cf. Is. 7:4–9; 8:11–15). Israel should only fear God and his wrath. So, even as the Lord assures them that Assyria must be the rod of his anger against them (10:5), he reaffirms that 'in a very little while my fury will come to an end, and my anger will be directed to their destruction' (v. 25).

God's power to do what he promises is illustrated by reference to two incidents from Israel's past. First, we are told that the Lord of hosts will wield against the Assyrians 'a whip, as when he struck Midian at the rock of Oreb' (10:26; cf. 9:4). God enabled Gideon and the men of Ephraim to defeat the oppressing Midianites and their leaders in a remarkable sequence of victories (Judg. 7:19–25). His victory over Assyria will be just like that. Second, we are told that Israel's deliverance will be like the miraculous escape from Egypt (Exod. 13 – 14), when their ancestors passed through the sea ('his staff will be over the sea, and he will lift it as he did in Egypt').

In the final analysis, God promises deliverance from the 'burden' which their own sin has brought upon them. 'In that day' of miraculous divine provision, 'his burden will depart from your shoulder, and his yoke from your neck'. This promise is reinforced with the rather comical picture of an ox which has eaten so well that the fat of its neck breaks open the yoke that restricts it ('the yoke will be broken because of the fat').[14]

Application

Isaiah's fundamental challenge is to fear God rather than the powers of evil, even though they 'strike with the rod and lift up their staff against you' (Is. 10:24; cf. 8:12–15). The only way to do this is to

---

14. NIV 'the yoke will be broken because you have grown so fat'.

understand God's purposes and trust him to act justly. Such trust comes from believing that he has revealed his will through the prophets and apostles he has chosen to be his mouthpiece. They give us a sure knowledge of what God has done in the past and a certainty about what he will do in the future. In other words, they point to the consistency of God in his dealings with us.

The gospel gives us the ultimate perspective on what God is doing in history. Isaiah's promise of the salvation of a remnant through the experience of divine justice is an example of the Scriptures 'preaching the gospel beforehand' (Gal. 3:8; cf. Rom. 1:1–2). But the suffering and unjust death of the Messiah at the hands of his own people is a turn of events not revealed until Isaiah 53. Christ's victory in and through that situation assures us that, if God is for us, nothing or no-one can 'separate us from the love of God which is in Christ Jesus our Lord' (Rom. 8:39).

When Isaiah relates the issues of faith and unbelief to everyday matters of political, national and personal survival, he gives us an important lesson. 'Faith is more than a means of justification; it is also an approach to the challenges of daily life, just as much for us as it was for those who faced the Assyrian threat. We are not only saved by faith; we live by it' (Webb; cf. 2 Cor. 5:7). Putting it another way, as we learn to trust in Christ alone for our salvation, we should learn to trust in God's justice, mercy and love in all the affairs of life. 'The life I now live in the flesh I live by faith in the Son of God, who loved me and gave himself for me' (Gal. 2:20).

3. Putting his judgment into effect (Is. 10:28–34)

[28]He has come to Aiath;
  he has passed through Migron;
    at Michmash he stores his baggage;
[29]they have crossed over the pass;
    at Geba they lodge for the night;
  Ramah trembles;
    Gibeah of Saul has fled.

[30]Cry aloud, O daughter of Gallim!

    Give attention, O Laishah!

    O Poor Anathoth!

[31]Madmenah is in flight;

    the inhabitants of Gebim flee for safety.

[32]This very day he will halt at Nob;

    he will shake his fist

    at the mount of the daughter of Zion,

    the hill of Jerusalem.

[33]Behold, the Lord God of hosts

    will lop the boughs with terrifying power;

  the great in height will be hewn down,

    and the lofty will be brought low.

[34]He will cut down the thickets of the forest

    with an axe,

    and Lebanon will fall by the Majestic One.

This passage presents in vivid, dramatic terms the advance of the Assyrian army on Jerusalem, as predicted (cf. 5:26–30). In the first part of this oracle (10:28–32), Isaiah speaks as though the advance has already begun. Various towns north of Jerusalem fall before the might of Assyria. Nothing can stop them until they 'halt at Nob'. At this point, Assyria will 'shake his fist at the mount of the daughter of Zion, the hill of Jerusalem'. In so doing, he will challenge the Lord who dwells in Zion and who is its true king (cf. Is. 36; Pss. 2; 46; 48).[15] In every way, the horror of the approaching judgment at the hands of the Assyrians is highlighted, and Isaiah makes it clear to 'the daughter of Zion' that there will be no escape.

    In the second part of this oracle, however (Is. 10:33–34), there is

---

15. Sennacherib advanced on Jerusalem in 701 BC from Lachish in the south-west. This shows that the prophecy of Is. 10:28–32 is not a literal prediction of the path of invasion but rather a poetic representation of the terrifying speed and efficiency with which the enemy would advance.

once again the assurance that Assyria will ultimately be restrained and defeated. 'The Lord God of hosts' will 'lop the boughs' of Assyria 'with terrifying power'.[16] 'The great in height', meaning Assyria in his arrogance and self-confidence, 'will be hewn down, and the lofty will be brought low'. This will be the end of 'the axe' that 'boasts over him who hews with it' (10:15)!

Application

'The Assyrians were sovereign until they met the Sovereign – and at the very moment when the threat is at the gates of Zion!' (Motyer). They met the one who judges all people equally and experienced the punishment as a nation which was due to them. Isaiah 36 – 37 records the actual outworking of the events predicted in chapter 10. In the last judgment, which this encounter prefigures, those who have opposed him and resisted the gracious offer of salvation in his Son, will fall before the Majestic One.

The last few verses of Isaiah 10 reinforce the message of the whole passage about God's strange work. 'While God may use evil people to accomplish his purpose, this does not in any way diminish their accountability' (Webb). We may continue to wonder at the way God works through human history to achieve his purposes. Some of our questions about God's sovereignty and human responsibility will never be answered. But Scripture encourages us to rejoice in 'the depth of the riches and wisdom and knowledge of God' and to say with Paul, 'How unsearchable are his judgments and how inscrutable his ways!' (Rom. 11:3). God's ultimate victory over sin, death and all the powers of the Evil One is achieved by the

---

16. Although some commentators such as Calvin, Kissane and Kaiser have taken 10:33–34 to refer to the lopping and felling of Judah, in preparation for the prophecy about a shoot coming forth from the stump of Jesse (11:1), this seems unlikely. Is. 10:28–34 parallels 10:5–27 in proclaiming the inevitability of the Assyrian attack but also the judgment of God against Assyria.

crucifixion and exaltation of his Son Jesus Christ (cf. John 12:31–33; Col. 1:19–20; 2:13–15; Heb. 2:14–18; 1 Pet. 3:18–22). A firm trust in the interplay of God's sovereignty and human responsibility in our present circumstances will preserve us from 'either denying the reality of evil or fearing that it will ultimately triumph' (Webb).

8 The Final Chapter
(Isaiah 11)

I used to like the sort of novel where the mystery is cunningly revealed at the end. But after a while I began to feel cheated. The butler could not have committed the murder because he was next door at the time! Since this information was held back until the last chapter, there was no way you could have guessed it. Much more satisfying is the novel which gives you enough clues along the way to anticipate the outcome.

God's plans for his people and the whole created order are gradually unfolded in Scripture like a mystery story. However, the revelation of this mystery is not artificial or contrived. Promises made centuries before are the basis for what is finally fulfilled. The wisdom, righteousness and grace of every strand of the story is made clear as the mystery is progressively unveiled.

Considering what we have read in Isaiah 7 – 10, you might call chapter 11 'the final chapter'. Of course, there is much more to be said about the future by Isaiah himself, let alone by the rest of the biblical writers. However, in a very real sense we are taken to the end of history in Isaiah 11 and are given an overview of everything

God intends to do. We are not completely surprised by further revelations, for they fit into the picture already given and show us how great and wonderful God is in achieving his purposes.

The prophet has so far predicted that the faithlessness of the Israelites and their leaders will lead to a devastating divine judgment, inflicted by the Assyrians. Only a remnant will be preserved in the south and the northern tribes will be devastated. But Isaiah 9:1–7 makes it clear that God will not give up on the house of David and his promise to bless his people through David's offspring. Light will shine in their darkness and they will be delivered from every form of oppression, when the coming king ushers in an eternal kingdom of justice, righteousness and peace.

In Isaiah 11 we learn more of this divine king from the house of David and the salvation he will accomplish. Motyer notes that there are two poems here (vv. 1–9; 12–16), separated by a prose section (vv. 10–11). The first poem deals with 'the king, the nature of his rule and the paradisal world where he reigns; the second deals with the world-wide people gathered to the Lord's banner'. Verse 10 effectively concludes the first poem and verse 11 introduces the second.[1]

For the purposes of exposition, however, I will divide the chapter thematically. We will first consider the endowments of the perfect king (vv. 1–2), then the justice of his perfect rule (vv. 3–5), the peace of his perfect rule (vv. 6–9) and finally the glory of his perfect rule (vv. 10–16). This king will bring blessing to all nations and a transformation of the whole created order. His rule will mark the climax of history and reverse all the effects of human sin. With an amazing foreshortening of the future, Isaiah portrays the person and work of the Lord Jesus Christ, both in his earthly ministry and in his second coming.

---

1. 11:10 forms an inclusion with 11:1–2 by repetition of similar terminology ('Jesse', a new word 'root' recalling 'shoot', 'resting place' recalling 'rest'). 11:11 lays the foundation for an inclusion with 11:15–16 (with the words 'hand', 'remnant', 'Assyria', 'Egypt').

1. The endowment of the perfect king (Is. 11:1–2)

¹There shall come forth a shoot from the stump of Jesse,
    and a branch from his roots shall bear fruit.
²And the Spirit of the LORD shall rest upon him,
    the Spirit of wisdom and understanding,
    the Spirit of counsel and might,
    the Spirit of knowledge and the fear of the LORD.

Assyria's swift and sudden destruction by God is portrayed in 10:33–34 in terms of bringing down its lofty trees. This happened in 609 BC, at the hands of the Babylonians, the Medes and the Persians. Nothing ever arose from the stump of Assyria again. Isaiah 11:1 implies that the ruling house of Judah will be similarly cut down. However, 'There shall come forth a shoot from the stump of Jesse, and a branch from his roots shall bear fruit.'

Reference to David's father Jesse suggests a radical restart of the whole divine plan to bless Israel through the emergence of a divinely appointed king. Among the many kings of Israel, David alone was called 'the son of Jesse' (e.g. 1 Sam. 20:27–33; 1 Kgs. 12:16). If Jesse produces another 'shoot' it must be another David, not simply another son of David (cf. Jer. 30:9; Ezek. 34:23–24; Hos. 3:5). New growth in the form of a 'shoot' from Jesse's stump, or a 'branch' from his roots, must 'come forth' by a special act of God.[2] This is so because of the failure of David's offspring to rule God's people appropriately and the consequent judgment on the house of David (cf. Is. 7:13).

A weak and faithless line of kings is to be replaced by one who is

---

2. The Hebrew for 'branch' in 11:1 is *nēṣer*. Another Hebrew word for 'branch' (*ṣemaḥ*) is used in 4:2, with reference to renewed Israel. The sequence in Is. 4 – 11 suggests that the renewal of Israel will take place because of the Spirit-anointed Davidic king. Branch imagery is used for the Messiah in Jer. 23:5; 33:15; Zech. 3:8; 6:12, using the same noun *ṣemaḥ*.

especially endowed by God's Spirit to bless his people (Is. 11:2; cf. 42:1; 59:21; 61:1). All the kings of Israel were anointed with oil and the expression 'the Lord's anointed' (Hebrew *māsiaḥ*) was a shorthand way of referring to them (e.g. 1 Sam. 24:10; Lam. 4:20). The term 'Messiah', with reference to the ultimate Ruler and Saviour, derives from this background and from the prediction of passages such as Isaiah 9 and 11. Significantly, David was not simply anointed with oil, but with God's Spirit, for his foundational role as king of Israel (1 Sam. 16:13; cf. 2 Sam. 23:1–2). Isaiah apparently takes this as the pattern for the one to come. What will be the outstanding characteristics of this new king?

Everything about him testifies to a supernatural endowment for his calling. As the one upon whom 'the Spirit of the Lord shall rest' (Is. 11:2), he will have 'the very breath of God about him' (Oswalt). The Spirit's presence and power will be manifested in the 'wisdom and understanding, counsel and might, knowledge and the fear of the Lord' that characterize his person and his rule. We are not to understand a variety of 'spirits' here but the several endowments of the one Spirit of God. 'Wisdom and understanding' are 'judicial and governmental attributes in Deuteronomy 1:13 and 1 Kings 3:9, 12' (Motyer). The words translated 'counsel and might' are rendered 'strategy and power for war' in Isaiah 36:5, suggesting 'the ability to devise a right course of action, coupled with the personal prowess to see it through' (Motyer). Foundational to all this will be a Spirit-given 'knowledge and the fear of the Lord'. Such 'knowledge' implies a distinctive relationship with the Lord and a life conformed to that relationship. Scripture affirms in several places that 'the fear of the Lord' is the way to true wisdom and knowledge (e.g. Prov. 1:7; Job 28:28), and this is to be supremely manifested in the Messiah.

In short, he will be able to perceive things correctly, make appropriate decisions for the welfare of God's people and carry them out with the right motivation and ability. These verses amplify what it means for the Messiah to be the 'Wonderful Counsellor' (Is. 9:6). Walking in the fear of the Lord, he will manifest the wisdom of God in every situation.

Application

Isaiah sees Davidic kingship in its ideal form as the pattern for the future, when God restores his people and fulfils his saving purpose for Israel and the nations. God's perfect rule will be exercised through his Spirit-anointed Son. This messianic typology, which involves development and escalation of kingdom perspectives from Israel's past, is picked up at many points in the New Testament to explain the significance of Jesus and his ministry.

So, for example, in the early chapters of Luke's Gospel, Jesus is introduced as 'Son of the Most High', to whom is given 'the throne of his father David' (1:32; cf. 2:11). As such, 'he will reign over the house of Jacob forever and of his kingdom there will be no end' (1:33). The Holy Spirit's role in his virginal conception is first highlighted (1:34–35) and then the Spirit's anointing and empowering for his earthly ministry is proclaimed (4:16–21, citing Is. 61:1–2).

Even in childhood, as he grew and became strong, he was 'filled with wisdom and the favour of God was upon him' (Luke 2:40, 52). Luke illustrates this with the story of Jesus engaging with the teachers in the temple (2:41–51). After Jesus announces in the synagogue at Nazareth that Isaiah 61:1–2 has been fulfilled, we see him proclaiming the good news of the kingdom of God, releasing those captive to demonic forces, healing the sick and acting with divine power in a whole range of situations. His perception, wisdom, motivation and authority demonstrate the empowering presence of the Spirit of the Lord.

In other words, the earthly ministry of Jesus Christ shows that he is the person in whom the prophecy of Isaiah 11:1–2 finds fulfilment. Exalted to the right hand of God (Acts 1:1–11; 2:32–36), he now lives and reigns to exercise the same wisdom, understanding, counsel and might in his relationship with us today. Everything the New Testament writers tell us about Jesus gives us confidence to trust in him as the promised Saviour-King, who inaugurates the end-time rule of God over Israel and the nations, with all the wonderful consequences outlined in the rest of Isaiah 11.

2. The justice of his perfect rule (Is. 11:3–5)

> ³And his delight shall be in the fear of the LORD.
>> He shall not judge by what his eyes see,
>> or decide disputes by what his ears hear,
> ⁴but with righteousness he shall judge the poor,
>> and decide with equity for the meek of the earth;
> and he shall strike the earth with the rod of his mouth,
>> and with the breath of his lips he shall kill the wicked.
> ⁵Righteousness shall be the belt of his waist,
>> and faithfulness the belt of his loins.

Isaiah turns from the Spirit's endowment of the perfect king to the way he exercises the gifts given to him. Inwardly, 'his delight shall be in the fear of the LORD' (11:3). 'The fear of the LORD' is again highlighted as the key motivation of his life. The critical task that is given to him is judgment. Isaiah has already declared that 'the LORD of hosts is exalted in justice, and the Holy God shows himself holy in righteousness' (5:16). The messianic king will manifest the justice of God in his eternal rule (cf. 16:5; Ps. 72).

Judging 'the poor' with 'righteousness' and deciding with equity 'for the meek of the earth' was a responsibility laid upon God's people in the Mosaic law (e.g. Exod. 23:6–11; Deut. 24:10–15, 17). But the leaders of Israel had failed to encourage and model this behaviour (cf. Is. 1:21–23; 3:12–15; 10:1–4). An ordinary king would 'judge by what his eyes see, or decide disputes by what his ears hear', but this Spirit-endowed ruler would have wisdom for judgment even beyond Solomon (cf. 1 Kings 3; 10:9). He would truly discern the needs of his people and be able to bring about the right solution for each individual. 'Here is a king in whose hands the concerns of the weakest will be safe' (Oswalt).

The claim that 'he shall strike the earth with the rod of his mouth, and with the breath of his lips he shall kill the wicked' (Is. 11:4) suggests again that he will be more than an ordinary mortal. Effective punishment is indicated. He will achieve God's purposes of judging 'the earth' with his bare word ('the rod of his mouth'). In the parallelism of the verse this is further defined as slaying 'the wicked' with 'the breath of his lips'. 'So the king's word is full of divine efficacy' (Motyer; cf. Ps. 33:6).

Garments express 'the inherent realities and capacities of a person and the purposes to which he commits himself ([Is.] 59:16–17; 61:10; Ps. 132:9, 16, 18)' (Motyer). So, when it says that 'righteousness shall be the belt of his waist, and faithfulness the belt of his loins', the implication is that 'righteousness' and 'faithfulness' are the controlling characteristics of his life (Is. 11:5). 'Righteousness' is the capacity for doing right in every circumstance. 'Faithfulness' means being dependable or true in every circumstance. These are characteristics of God 'upon which the whole biblical understanding of life is built' (Oswalt; e.g. 5:16, 'righteousness'; 65:16, 'faithfulness'). What the people of Israel saw in their God would be manifested in their king. These verses amplify what it means for him to be 'Mighty God' and 'Everlasting Father' (9:6).

Application

When Jesus proclaimed, 'The kingdom of God is at hand', what kind of kingdom did he envisage? Isaiah gives us the answer. The kingdom of God is ruled by one who delights in the fear of the Lord, judges with perfect insight and righteousness, and manifests the faithfulness of God to his people in every way.

In the Gospels, we see again how Jesus fulfils the vision of Isaiah. First, he revealed that his delight was in the fear of the Lord, when he declared, 'My food is to do the will of him who sent me and to accomplish his work' (John 4:34). Second, he demonstrated a perception of people and their needs beyond what his eyes saw or his ears heard (e.g. John 2:24–25; 4:16–18). Third, such discernment enabled him to bring appropriate words of warning or encouragement in each particular case (e.g. John 3:1–21; 4:7–26). Whether dealing with opponents or the needy, with outcasts such as 'tax collectors and sinners' or the religious authorities of his day, Jesus manifested the righteousness and faithfulness of God to each individual (e.g. John 5 – 9). Fourth, he showed how the final judgment of humanity would be conducted with righteousness and faithfulness (e.g. John 3:31–36; 5:19–47).

Such New Testament evidence gives us confidence about the way the Lord Jesus will accomplish that final judgment. God has 'fixed a day on which he will judge the world in righteousness by a man whom he has appointed and of this he has given assurance to all by raising him from the dead' (Acts 17:31). Absolute justice demands absolute knowledge. The fairness and effectiveness of that judgment is proclaimed by the prophecy of Isaiah and illustrated in the life and ministry of Jesus.

3. The peace of his perfect rule (Is. 11:6–9)

> ⁶The wolf shall dwell with the lamb
>   and the leopard shall lie down with the young goat,
>   and the calf and the lion and the fattened
>   calf together;
>   and a little child shall lead them.
> ⁷The cow and the bear shall graze;
>   their young shall lie down together;
>   and the lion shall eat straw like the ox.
> ⁸The nursing child shall play over the hole of the cobra,
>   and the weaned child shall put his hand on the
>   adder's den.
> ⁹They shall not hurt or destroy
>   in all my holy mountain;
>   for the earth shall be full of the knowledge of the LORD
>   as the waters cover the sea.

Messiah's rule will bring perfect peace, involving a transformation of the whole created order (cf. Is. 35:9; 65:25). Such imagery suggests a restoration of the paradise of Eden (cf. Gen. 2:5–25), by reversing the effects of the fall (cf. Gen. 3:8–24). This leads on to the revelation that the messianic salvation will extend to the nations.

God will be known and his rule experienced everywhere, 'for the earth shall be full of the knowledge of the Lord as the waters cover the sea'. Renewal of the creation and renewal of those who inhabit it go together in this prophecy.

Perfect safety for the vulnerable in the animal world is first highlighted. 'The wolf shall dwell with the lamb and the leopard shall lie down with the young goat, and the calf and the lion and the fattened calf together' (Is. 11:6). Predators and prey will be reconciled. Mortal enemies will dwell together in absolute harmony. Moreover, wild and terrifying animals will depend upon the leadership of a child, 'the one supposedly least able to control their voracious instincts' (Oswalt). Restoration of humanity's proper dominion over the created order is suggested by the prediction that 'a little child shall lead them' (cf. Gen. 1:26–28; Ps. 8:6–8). When this happens, the created order will be transformed.

Isaiah's message of reconciliation and peace is reinforced in 11:7, with the promise that 'the cow and the bear shall graze; their young shall lie down together; and the lion shall eat straw like the ox'. The strong will no longer oppress and destroy the weak. Moreover, there is even the suggestion that the enmity between the woman's seed and the serpent will be removed: 'the nursing child shall play over the hole of the cobra, and the weaned child shall put his hand on the adder's den' (Is. 11:8; cf. Gen. 3:15). By implication, death itself will be defeated by the sovereign, transforming power of God (cf. Is. 25:7–8).

Finally, there is the straightforward claim that 'they shall not hurt or destroy in all my holy mountain' (Is. 11:9). The next clause makes it clear that God's 'holy mountain' is equivalent to 'the earth', which is 'full of the knowledge of the Lord'. 'When the true order of creation is restored the whole earth is the Lord's hill, indwelt by his holiness' (Motyer). This comprehensive statement must surely include humanity as well as the animals. From a biblical point of view, it is humanity's rebellion against God that leads to the disorder and pain, futility and death that characterize life outside the Garden of Eden (Gen. 3:8–24). When the true knowledge of God is spread among the nations, implying a restoration of relationship with God, there will be a renewal of the whole created order.

In biblical theology, God makes a covenant with Abraham and his offspring in order to bless all the families of the earth (Gen. 12:1–3). He rescues the Israelites from bondage in Egypt and brings them to himself at Mount Sinai (Exod. 19:1–6). At that 'holy mountain', they meet with God and learn how they may engage with him and be his holy people. In due course, they are given the promised land, with Zion as the 'holy mountain' at its centre (cf. Deut. 12:1–14; 2 Sam. 5:6–10). There the temple is built and people are commanded to meet with God and to renew their relationship with him (1 Kgs. 8 – 9). There they are told how to live under his word and to demonstrate to the nations what it means to be a people possessed and blessed by God.

Prophets like Isaiah, however, condemn the faithlessness of God's people and are particularly scathing about the hypocrisy of those who worship at the temple but lead lives that are totally abhorrent to God (e.g. Is. 1:10–20). Israel cannot be a channel of blessing to the nations while she remains in rebellion against God. So God promises to renew the worship of Israel and make 'the mountain of the Lord' the place to which the nations are drawn (2:1–3). When 'the word of the Lord' goes out from Jerusalem, the nations will learn to 'walk in his paths' and perfect peace will be experienced (2:4).

Isaiah 11 picks up this theme with the promise that 'the earth shall be full of the knowledge of the Lord as the waters cover the sea'. The transformation of which the prophet speaks will take place because 'the knowledge of the Lord' will spread everywhere. And the context suggests that it is the Messiah's wisdom, righteousness and faithfulness that make this spread of 'the knowledge of the Lord' possible. These verses amplify what it means for him to be 'Prince of Peace' (Is. 9:6).

Application

Isaiah indicates that human attempts to achieve a just and lasting peace are ultimately futile. Only God can achieve the transformation envisaged here, by filling the earth with a true knowledge of his character and will and by removing the enmity that keeps us from God and separates us from one another. The prophet draws together various images from the creation narratives and Israel's redemptive history to develop and expand the typology introduced in the opening verses of this chapter. The rule of the Spirit-anointed Messiah will bring about the promised reconciliation and transformation.

The New Testament proclaims that a great act of reconciliation or peace-making has been achieved by the sacrificial death of the Jesus Christ (Rom. 5:1–11; 2 Cor. 5:17–21; Eph. 2:11–22). God has been pleased to 'reconcile to himself all things, whether on earth or in heaven, making peace by the blood of his cross' (Col. 1:20). The knowledge of God's saving work and the experience of the Messiah's peace come to the world through the preaching of the gospel.

In the Acts of the Apostles, Luke shows how 'the word of God' or the gospel began to have a transforming effect in Jerusalem, in all Judea and Samaria, and finally 'to the end of the earth' (Acts 1:8; cf. Is. 49:6). So also today, those who repent and trust in Christ can have their sins blotted out and experience 'times of refreshing from the presence of the Lord' (Acts 3:19–20). But they must wait for the consummation of God's plans, as portrayed in Isaiah 11:6–9 and 65:17–25. This will happen when God sends his Christ again, 'whom heaven must receive until the time for restoring all the things about which God spoke by the mouth of his holy prophets long ago' (Acts 3:21).

Given these prophetic promises and the fact that Jesus has already accomplished the definitive act of restoration by his death and resurrection, the New Testament urges us to live in patient, persevering hope. Paul emphasizes this in Romans 8:18–25, where he talks about the creation being 'set free from its bondage to decay', to share in 'the freedom of the glory of the children of

God'. The whole of the Revelation to John has this focus, with the concluding chapters describing the perfection of 'a new heaven and a new earth', using an array of images from the prophets. We can be even more sure than believers in Old Testament times that God will achieve his final goal because of what he has already accomplished through the victory of the Lord Jesus, the pouring out of his Spirit and the spread of his gospel in all the world.

4. The glory of his perfect rule (Is. 11:10–16)

[10]In that day the root of Jesse, who shall stand as a signal for the peoples – of him shall the nations enquire, and his resting-place shall be glorious.

[11]In that day the Lord will extend his hand yet a second time to recover the remnant that remains of his people, from Assyria, from Egypt, from Pathros, from Cush, from Elam, from Shinar, from Hamath, and from the coastlands of the sea.

[12]He will raise a signal for the nations
and will assemble the banished of Israel,
and gather the dispersed of Judah
from the four corners of the earth.
[13]The jealousy of Ephraim shall depart,
and those who harass Judah shall be cut off;
Ephraim shall not be jealous of Judah,
and Judah shall not harass Ephraim.
[14]But they shall swoop down on the shoulder of the
Philistines in the west,
and together they shall plunder the people of the east.
They shall put out their hand against Edom and Moab,
and the Ammonites shall obey them.
[15]And the LORD will utterly destroy
the tongue of the Sea of Egypt,
and will wave his hand over the River
with his scorching breath,
and strike it into seven channels,

and he will lead people across in sandals.
16And there will be a highway from Assyria
          for the remnant that remains of his people,
      as there was for Israel
          when they came up from the land of Egypt.

'In that day' (v. 10) signifies the same time as the events in verses 1–9. The reference is to the end time, even though Isaiah's predictions arise out of the immediate historical situation in which the people of his generation found themselves (see comment on v. 16 below). 'In that day the root of Jesse' shall 'stand as a signal for the peoples'. He is the one in whom the prophecies of 2:2–4 and 4:2–5 will be fulfilled. Portrayed as 'a signal for the peoples', the Messiah will be like a great warrior-king with a banner, calling the nations to join him in the enjoyment of his glorious victory.[3] In this vast, end-time assembly, Webb observes two 'rings':

> In the outer ring (10) will be the Gentile nations, who will at last come to recognise the Lord's rule. In the inner circle (11–16) will be the people of God, at last finally delivered from their enemies. But this inner group will not be passive. They will participate in the Lord's rule over the outer group (14).

Isaiah promises that 'of him shall the nations enquire'. Israelites, who did not 'enquire of the Lord' (9:13), will be part of a great multitude who now seek the Messiah. 'The knowledge of the Lord' shall fill the earth because the nations seek it from 'the root of Jesse'. So the Gentiles will be brought in by the Messiah to be blessed with Israel and share in Israel's salvation (cf. Gen. 12:3 and subsequent promises such as Is. 19:23–25; 56:6–8).

---

3. The image of the Lord raising a signal for the nations is used differently in 5:26, to indicate a gathering of the nations to be the agents of his judgment against rebellious Israel.

Isaiah also promises that 'his resting place shall be glorious'. The term 'resting place' is significantly used for the promised land, where the people of Israel were given rest from their enemies to dwell in safety with God in their midst (Deut. 12:9–10; Josh. 1:13; 21:44; Ps. 95:11). The ark of the Lord finally came to rest in Jerusalem, showing that Mount Zion was specifically God's 'resting place' (Ps. 132:8, 14). There God's glory was revealed (1 Kgs. 8:1–11). So when the Messiah creates the perfect peace envisaged in Isaiah 11:6–9, 'his resting place shall be glorious'. It will be the fulfilment of the typology of ark and promised land together, because God will be there in all his glory (cf. 4:5; 6:1–4). Here is another way in which it is suggested that the Messiah's coming will be the coming of God himself.

'In that day' (Is. 11:11) again signifies the end time mentioned in verses 1–9. However, this prose verse introduces the concluding poem in Isaiah 11, where the focus is on the recovery of 'the remnant that remains of his people' (vv. 11, 16). This group is further defined as 'the banished of Israel' and 'the dispersed of Judah' (v. 12). When the Messiah comes, the remnant of the people of God will be recovered 'from Assyria, from Egypt, from Pathros, from Cush, from Elam, from Shinar, from Hamath, and from the coastlands of the sea' (v. 11). Indeed, it will be gathered 'from the four corners of the earth' (v. 12). Release from captivity is implied. Israel must be saved so that the nations can be blessed with Israel.

The nations mentioned here and in verses 14–16 represent the enemies of Israel throughout her history. Release 'from Assyria' doubtless comes first (v. 11), because that would be the most pressing need in view of Isaiah's predictions of attack by the Assyrians (10:5–12, 28–34). Rescue from captivity by the Assyrians is compared with the exodus 'from the land of Egypt' (11:15–16).[4] But a wider exodus from a world-wide dispersion has already

---

4. Return from captivity in Babylon is later portrayed in similar terms as a second or new exodus (Is. 43:14–21; 50:2–3). But this deliverance in history

been signified (vv. 11–12). Isaiah's vision in this passage is for a comprehensive salvation of the remnant of Israel.

The Lord will accomplish this by extending 'his hand yet a second time' (v. 12). Such language emphasizes the personal action of God, as in the exodus (cf. Exod. 3:19–20; 6:1; 13:3; Deut. 6:21). He will do this by drawing them to the Messiah, through whom he ushers in 'a reign of safety and security to which the weary exiles may come streaming in return' (Oswalt).

God's assembling and re-establishing of 'the banished of Israel' and 'the dispersed of Judah' (Is. 11:12) will necessitate a dramatic transformation of the people. 'Ephraim shall not be jealous of Judah, and Judah shall not harass Ephraim' (v. 13). Unity and brotherly love will be God's gift to the survivors of the northern and southern kingdoms alike. This will stop them fighting each other and enable them to 'swoop down on the shoulder of the Philistines to the west and together they shall plunder the people of the east' (v. 14). 'The reconstituted people of God (12–13) become the agents in the spreading kingdom' (Motyer). But the image of God's people engaging in military conquest is not to be pressed literally. The preceding passage has suggested that the Messiah's rule will be established by his own righteousness and faithfulness. Messiah's people become the agents of his kingdom as they enjoy the benefits of his victory and live as the reconciled people of God under his rule.

It is important to note again that the nations that are mentioned in this chapter represent the enemies of God's people collectively. 'The Philistines in the west' (v. 14) had ceased to have any national identity in Isaiah's time. Other historic enemies such as 'Edom and Moab' are mentioned alongside 'the Ammonites, Egypt' and the great contemporary enemy 'Assyria'. God's sovereignty over all these enemies is proclaimed. His great victory over 'the Sea of Egypt' at the time of the exodus is the pattern that will be repeated.

---

was only a foretaste or anticipation of the ultimate deliverance through Christ, to which the book of Isaiah consistently points.

He will 'wave his hand over the River with his scorching breath,[5] and strike it into seven channels', enabling him to 'lead people across in sandals' (v. 15).

The final picture is of 'a highway from Assyria' for the remnant of Israel, as there was a way through the desert for God's people 'when they came up from the land of Egypt' (v. 16). The end-time focus of this passage makes it clear that the fulfilment was not even in the return of the scattered Israelites after the Babylonian exile. This was a small anticipation of the final restoration in Christ. Isaiah 11 as a whole suggests that the Messiah himself is the way of salvation. He is the Spirit-anointed judge and deliverer, who rescues and restores the remnant of Israel and draws the nations to share in the benefits of the renewed creation, which is his glorious resting place.

Application

So the mystery is out! The final chapter of God's plan for creation has been revealed, at least in outline. We know that the Spirit-anointed 'shoot from the root of Jesse' is central to that plan. We know that his rule will be one of perfect righteousness and faithfulness. We know that his kingdom will bring perfect peace – the reconciliation of all things – because 'the earth shall be full of the knowledge of the Lord'. Now finally we discover that this involves 'the root of Jesse' drawing all people to himself (cf. John 12:32). Israelites will be reconciled to one another and the reconstituted people of God will become the agents of his reconciling rule to others.

The book of Acts shows how this began to be fulfilled. The gospel came to the Jews first and brought many thousands to faith in Jesus as the Christ (Acts 1 – 3). But with this came mounting opposition from the leaders of Israel and others (Acts 4 – 7). Persecution led to the scattering of many Jewish believers and the taking of the gospel to Samaria and the nations (8 – 28). Many

---

5. The Euphrates river is probably intended.

Gentiles were drawn into the community of faith with Jewish Christians. But even at the end of Acts, Paul is found urging Jews in Rome not harden their hearts and miss out on the Messiah and the salvation he brings (28:17–28). The apostle quotes God's address to the prophet in Isaiah 6:9–10 as part of his warning.

So Acts ends with the story of salvation incomplete and with many still resisting the claims of Christ. The apostle Paul reflects on this in his letter to the Romans and reveals that 'a partial hardening has come upon Israel, until the fullness of the Gentiles has come in, and then all Israel will be saved' (Rom. 11:25–26). The context suggests that this will happen at the end of this age, when Christ returns (note vv. 26–27, citing Is. 59:20–21). The full number of God's elect among the Gentiles and in Israel will ultimately be saved.

God has not given up on Israel, even though many Jews deny the messiahship of Jesus and reject the gospel. Paul's point in these chapters is to assure us that the word of God has not failed, that God's process of election continues, as he persistently holds out his hands to 'a disobedient and contrary people' (Rom. 10:21, citing Is. 65:2). Israel's 'trespass' has made it possible for the messianic salvation to come to the Gentiles (Rom. 11:11). But even as God continues to be gracious to the Gentiles in this way, his intention is to 'make Israel jealous' and thus save some of them (Rom. 11:11, 14, alluding to Deut. 32:21).

As we read Isaiah 11 in the light of what God has already accomplished, we can rejoice and give thanks (cf. Is. 12). At the same time, we should recognize that we have a part to play in the continuing story. We must point people to Christ as the only one in whom salvation for all nations is to be found. Furthermore, no matter what struggles we may have to endure, we have a hope that is firm and secure. What God has already achieved in Christ is the guarantee that everything promised in the Scriptures will be fulfilled.

In the end, Messiah's 'resting place shall be glorious', not simply because God will be in the midst of his people for ever but because his reconciling and redeeming purposes will be perfectly fulfilled in the new creation. Ungodliness will be banished from Israel and the promised remnant will be saved. The nations will also be drawn to Messiah's banner in great numbers and all opposition to his rule will cease. God's glory will be fully and finally seen in the way he defeats his enemies and reverses the effects of humanity's rebellion against him.

9 Meaningful Praise
(Isaiah 12)

Praise is an important aspect of what we do when we meet together as Christians. It is a way of letting the word of Christ 'dwell' in us richly, as we teach and admonish one another 'in all wisdom, singing psalms and hymns and spiritual songs', with thankfulness in our hearts to God (Col. 3:16). Indeed, Spirit-filled Christians are characterized as 'addressing one another in psalms and hymns and spiritual songs, singing and making melody to the Lord with all your heart, giving thanks always and for everything to God the Father in the name of our Lord Jesus Christ' (Eph. 5:18–20).

Sadly, however, praise can become a source of division amongst Christians, rather than a way of honouring God and building up his church. Singing can be used primarily to create an atmosphere or to play on the emotions. Music style can become the issue rather than words. Praise can be empty of meaning and substance. Mind-numbing repetition of even the best words can be confused with true worship and hinder the edification of the church, rather than advance it.

Scripture gives us many examples of praise to guide us in composing or selecting appropriate material for use in our churches today. Apart from Old Testament psalms or the songs in the Revelation to John, praise occurs at several significant points in the history of God's people, focusing on the mighty acts of God in saving his people and judging his enemies.[1] Such songs enable us to consider the character and purpose of God-honouring praise.

Isaiah 12 concludes the account of the Messiah's kingdom, which began in 11:1. It also concludes the first main division of the book in ways that will become clear as we explore the song in detail. 'Chapter 12 celebrates both the rule of the Messiah and God dwelling among his people; they are one and the same thing. This is the goal towards which both the Zion prophecies of chapters 2 and 4 and the messianic prophecies of chapters 9 and 11 point' (Webb).

There are actually two songs in chapter 12 (vv. 1–2, 4–6), each introduced with the words 'you will say in that day'. Between the songs there is a promise (v. 3, 'With joy you will draw water from the wells of salvation'), providing a clear context for the praise that is offered. This central verse also marks a transition from personal to corporate praise.

1. Praise for God's deliverance (Is. 12:1–2)

> [1]You will say in that day:
>> 'I will give thanks to you, O LORD,
>>> for though you were angry with me,
>> your anger turned away,
>>> that you might comfort me.

> [2]'Behold, God is my salvation;
>> I will trust, and will not be afraid;
> for the LORD GOD is my strength and my song,
>> and he has become my salvation.'

---

1. E.g. Exod. 15:1–18; Judg. 5:1–31; 1 Sam. 2:1–10; Is. 12:1–6; 25:1–5, 9–12; 26:1–19; Luke 1:46–55, 68–79; 2:29–32.

The introductory expression 'You will say' is in the singular in Hebrew and the song itself is worded in the first person singular ('I will give thanks to you, O LORD ... though you were angry with me'), providing a very personal expression of thanksgiving and trust. The form of this song reminds us that, although genuine praise ought to be offered by God's people collectively, it must find individual expression in the life of every true believer. Even when we are singing together, each must be able to affirm his or her personal trust and gratitude to the Lord with appropriate words.

The phrase 'in that day' was previously used of the approaching divine judgment (e.g. 2:11; 3:18; 7:18, 20–21, 23). But it has also been used to refer to the time when the remnant returns to the Lord (10:20), when the burden of Assyria is lifted from Judah's shoulders (10:27), and when the root of Jesse draws the remnant of Israel and the nations to share in his glorious resting place (11:10–11). So, as Isaiah looks forward, he conveys a complex picture of several events, focused in a single 'day'. Ultimately, he looks to the day of the messianic salvation, but sees other features of the immediate future anticipating this in various ways. Like someone looking through a telescope, he sees distant events close up, but sees also the immediate future in the foreground, linked to those distant events.

The first thing for which believers would give thanks 'in that day' is deliverance from divine judgment ('for though you were angry with me, your anger turned away'). God's people would acknowledge that the anger of the Lord directed at them collectively was also directed to them personally. None could escape responsibility for Israel's failure to please God and fulfil his purpose for them. But the time would come when they could acknowledge that the anger of the Lord had been satisfied and had 'turned away' from them. In 10:25 this hope is expressed in terms of God's fury through the Assyrian attack coming to an end and then being directed to the destruction of the enemy. Significantly, it is the Lord who both expresses his anger and who also turns it away. There is nothing that human beings can do to appease God's anger or to escape from it by their own cunning.

The second thing for which believers would give thanks 'in that day' is God's comfort ('that you might comfort me'). 'The angry God is finally the only source of comfort' (Webb). Indeed, the purpose of turning away his anger is to bring his comfort to those he loves. The word translated 'comfort' was earlier used to describe God getting 'relief' from his enemies by punishing them (1:24). Here the notion is that the Lord gives relief to those who have encountered his own anger. In other words, comfort is not just a warm feeling of being loved but the experience of being delivered from God's righteous judgment (cf. 40:1–2; 49:13; 61:1–2). 'Since God's anger is based on a just cause, and is not the result of personal pique, the comfort of God comes only after sin and iniquity have been punished' (Oswalt).

At this stage in Isaiah's prophecy there is no complete explanation of the way his anger can be satisfied and his comfort offered. The Assyrian invasion and later the Babylonian exile were terrible punishments for sin. But these did not automatically restore the people to fellowship with God nor introduce the blessings of the messianic salvation. Something more was needed because of the seriousness of their situation under the curse of God (cf. Deut. 28:15–68). The ultimate revelation comes in Isaiah 53, where we are introduced to an individual who can take the place of God's guilty people. Only the affliction of the suffering servant can bring them 'peace' with God and only 'with his stripes' can they be 'healed' (v. 5). His death will be accepted by God as an atoning sacrifice for others, since 'the LORD has laid on him the iniquity of us all' (v. 6).

In summary, Isaiah looks forward to the day when each believer will be able to acknowledge that 'God is my salvation' (Is. 12:2). There is no salvation apart from God, who saves by his own mighty actions and who 'is' salvation for all who rely on him. This verse echoes the song of Moses and the people of Israel, when they experienced God's deliverance through the exodus from Egypt: 'The LORD is my strength and my song, and he has become my salvation' (Exod. 15:2). In both contexts, thanksgiving for the rescue of God's people collectively is expressed in individual and personal terms. Isaiah's echo of the Song of Moses suggests a salvation of equal, or even greater significance for the people of God. According to Isaiah 12:1, it is a definitive deliverance from divine judgment so as to enjoy the 'comfort' of God. The full dimensions of that comfort are set out in the picture of the Messiah's kingdom in Isaiah 11.

'In that day', believers will be able to say, 'I will trust, and will not be afraid'. This was what Isaiah was challenging Ahaz to say (7:2–9). This is what characterizes the true children of God (8:11–18). Such confidence for the future is bound up with knowing God as a source of power and joy in the present ('my strength and my song'). This in turn is bound up with knowing him as Saviour in the past ('he has become my salvation'). So the three tenses of experience – past, present and future – are bound together in Isaiah's song and form a helpful model for thinking about praise and its relation to the life of faith.

Application

Isaiah looks to the time when God's people will trust him and not be afraid, rejoicing in the comfort and salvation that he has brought to them. Such a response will be possible only when God takes the initiative and acts graciously to rescue and renew them. Isaiah 11 shows that he will do this through the promised ruler, anointed by his Spirit.

For Christians, it is clear that the Messiah has come in Jesus and his rule has begun. Zechariah's song celebrates this at the beginning of Luke's Gospel (1:68–79), proclaiming that God has raised up 'a horn of salvation' for Israel 'in the house of his servant David'. This is in fulfilment of what the prophets predicted, based on the provisions of the original covenant with Abraham. Zechariah seems to be particularly influenced by the perspectives of Isaiah. God will deliver his people from their enemies, so that they can serve him 'without fear, in holiness and righteousness before him all our days'. But the heart of the matter is 'the forgiveness of their sins', light instead of darkness, life instead of death, and the enjoyment of a God-given peace. In Luke 2:29–32, Simeon affirms that this salvation will be for 'all peoples', not simply for Israel.

In the Song of Zechariah, as in the Song of Isaiah, we see that God-honouring praise puts the focus on God and what he has done for us, not primarily on the human experience of salvation and its consequences. But there is nothing quite like the style and form of Isaiah 12:1–2 in the New Testament. Here we have an expression of personal thanksgiving for salvation which can be easily applied to our situation in Christ. So we can use Isaiah's words to praise him for turning away his anger from us in the death of the Lord Jesus and comforting us with the reconciliation we have in him (cf. Rom. 5:1–11). We can affirm that in Christ, 'God is my salvation', and on that basis continue to trust and not be afraid (cf. Rom. 8:31–39).

2. Praise for God's enduring presence (Is. 12:3–6)

[3]With joy you will draw water from the wells of salvation. [4]And you will say in that day:

> 'Give thanks to the LORD,
>   call upon his name,
>   make known his deeds among the peoples,
>   proclaim that his name is exalted.

> [5]'Sing praises to the LORD, for he has done gloriously;
>   let this be made known in all the earth.
> [6]Shout, and sing for joy, O inhabitant of Zion,
>   for great in your midst is the Holy One of Israel.'

As noted previously, verse 3 marks a transition from singular 'you' to the plural and introduces the second song. This verse makes it clear that the second song is also about the enjoyment of God's salvation, now expressed in a corporate and collective way. 'The theme is salvation, and the occasion is salvation experienced in full measure, like water drawn at will from inexhaustible wells. The result is joy, and it is this joy to which the songs give expression' (Webb). Water imagery expresses the abundant provision of God for his people (e.g. Is. 33:21; 35:6–7; 44:3; 55:1).

The first song begins with a direct address to God (12:1, 'I will give thanks to you O Lord'), and moves to address the self to 'trust and not be afraid' (v. 2). The second song is in the form of an exhortation to other believers to 'give thanks to the Lord' and to praise him so that his deeds are 'made known in all the earth'. This second form of praise is common in the Psalms and is not to be considered inferior because it is more indirect (e.g. Pss. 29; 33; 47; 66; 95). In human relationships we praise people face to face, but also when we talk about them to others. So it must be with God. A vital part of praise is proclaiming the character and deeds of God to one another, as we urge each other to join in acknowledging his greatness and goodness.

Four different imperatives together describe what God's people are to do (Is. 12:4; cf. Ps. 105:1). 'Give thanks to the Lord' implies specific acknowledgment of the blessings received from him, as outlined in Isaiah 12:1. 'Call upon his name' means invoking God by using his name (cf. Gen. 12:8). 'God has made himself known by name, i.e. revealed himself and summed up the revelation in a significant name' (Motyer). Believers can approach him in the light of that revelation, asking him for help and thus continuing to trust him and not be afraid (as in Is. 12:2). 'Make known his deeds among the peoples' means advertising his saving work to all, by proclaiming what he has done. 'Far from trusting in the nations for her own salvation, Israel is intended to be the vehicle whereby the nations can come to God' (Oswalt).

Isaiah's earlier vision was of the nations coming to experience the salvation of Israel because the word of the Lord goes out from Jerusalem (2:2–4). From 12:4 we may say that this happens because the people of God 'make known his deeds among the peoples' and 'proclaim that his name is exalted'. This last expression suggests that his character as the exalted, sovereign Lord is made known as his deeds are rehearsed. 'So long as the world seeks to exalt itself, it pursues a will-of-the-wisp that will eventually exhaust it. But if it will recognize his unique glory, it will find well-being and gracious

exaltation streaming from him who alone can give them (60:13, 15)'
(Oswalt).

The second stanza begins with the exhortation to 'sing praises
to the Lord, for he has done gloriously' (Is. 12:5). This and the
following verse remind us that singing is a marvellous way of praising
and thanking God because it helps us to express our joy more fully
(v. 6, 'shout and sing for joy'). Praise in Scripture is clearly meant to
be a vigorous and delightful activity (cf. Pss. 149 – 150), not a half-
hearted miserable duty! And what the Lord has 'done gloriously',
is not to be kept a secret. It is to be 'made known in all the
earth'.

The people of God are personified in a single individual
('O inhabitant of Zion'), who is exhorted to 'shout and sing for joy'
(Is. 12:6). 'Zion' is where the redeemed will live, when Isaiah's
vision of the future is fulfilled (4:2–6),[2] and from 'Zion' God's
revelation will go out to the nations (2:3). The Lord's glorious deeds
of judgment and salvation will establish his presence in Zion, so
that all will be able to say, 'great in your midst is the Holy One of
Israel'.

Isaiah's chapter of praise finishes by reaffirming two important
notes sounded earlier in his prophecy. 'The Holy One of Israel' was
the one who revealed himself to the prophet and commissioned
him to make his purposes known. At the heart of that revelation
was the divine intention to save a remnant of Israel through
judgment and to re-establish his kingly rule in 'Zion'. In some
passages this is clearly linked to the coming of the Messiah but in
others it is more generally a promise of God's presence, to judge and
to save. So the central theme of these chapters is 'Immanuel' – God

---

2. However, we noted in connection with 11:9 that the image of Zion or
   God's 'holy mountain' merges with 'the earth' or the whole land. In
   65:17–25 the renewed Jerusalem merges with the predicted 'new
   heavens and a new earth'. The holy city represents perfect community,
   where God and his people dwell together under his perfect rule.

with us, to renew his covenant and his saving purposes for Israel and the whole created order.

Application

Meaningful praise glorifies God and edifies the church. Indeed, exhortations to praise are as important as direct words of thanksgiving to God because they contain reasons for praise, highlighting the very things that are great and wonderful about God. The church is edified by biblically based praise because it is a means by which we encourage one another to keep on trusting God and to honour him in every aspect of our lives.

Meaningful praise can also be a way of proclaiming God's character and deeds to unbelievers so that they can acknowledge him. Such praise can be expressed in testimony, prophecy and preaching, as well as in singing. The apostle Paul warns about the importance of speaking and singing in church in a way that can be understood by all, including outsiders or unbelievers who may enter the meeting (1 Cor. 14:13–25). Such a person may be convicted of sin, fall on his face and worship God, because he is convicted of the reality of God and his presence amongst his people.

So Isaiah's exhortation to 'shout and sing for joy', because 'great in your midst is the Holy One of Israel', has a fulfilment in the gathering of Christians to minister to one another and to 'sing praises to the Lord'. Praising God together in the assembly of his people can also be a powerful encouragement to praise him in everyday contacts with unbelievers, as we 'make known his deeds' and proclaim his character (cf. Col. 4:5–6; Heb. 13:15; 1 Pet. 3:15–16).

Finally, we can see from the Revelation to John that the redeemed in heaven sing the praises of God and the Lamb who saved them (e.g. 4:11; 5:9–12; 11:17–18; 15:3–4). They are those who experience the ultimate fulfilment of Isaiah's prophecy about the Holy One being in the midst of his people. With these songs, the victory of Christ is proclaimed and the final drama of God's plan is unfolded. As Christians on earth share the praises of heaven, they anticipate the enjoyment of that final assembly of God's people. They are encouraged to live patient, faithful and godly lives, as they wait for the final judgment and the new creation.[3]

---

3. I have written more fully on the songs in 'Revelation and their relevance to Christian worship' in *Engaging with God: A Biblical Theology of Worship* (Leicester: Apollos; Grand Rapids, MI: Eerdmans, 1992), pp. 270–279.

Index of Scripture References